PIERCING HUMAN EXPERIENCE

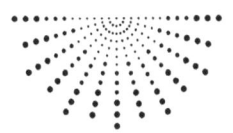

PIERCING HUMAN EXPERIENCE

BASED ON MANDUKYA KARIKA

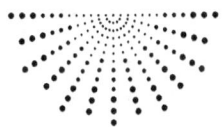

TUSHAR CHOKSI

ADVAYA PRESS

Copyright © 2021 by Tushar Choksi

All rights reserved.

No part of this book may be reproduced in any form or by any electronic or mechanical means, including information storage and retrieval systems, without written permission from the author, except for the use of brief quotations in a book review.

Printed in the United States of America

First Printing, 2021

ISBN: 978-0-578-70160-8

Front cover image by Atri & Jinal Choksi

Advaya Press

यस्तु सर्वाणि भूतानि आत्मन्येवानुपश्यति।
सर्वभूतेषु चात्मानं ततो न विजुगुप्सते ॥

I bow down to Shrinathji (Ishvara)

with love,

The Indwelling Self of All

CONTENTS

Foreword ... ix
Preface ... xiii
Acknowledgments ... xxi

Part I
SEARCHING THE SELF

1. Need for Piercing Human Experience ... 3
2. Defining the Mind ... 9
3. Discriminating between Real and Unreal ... 11
4. Searching the Self of the Human Being ... 15

Part II
WORLD AS OBJECTS

5. Waking State - World as Physical Objects ... 21
6. Dream State - World as Subtle Objects ... 25

Part III
OBJECTS AS MIND

7. Learning from Dream State ... 31
8. Waking and Dream State are the Same ... 35
9. Identity as Common Mind ... 41
10. Cause of the Waking and Dream State ... 43
11. Inactive State of Mind ... 47
12. Identity as Ishvara ... 51

Part IV
MIND AS WITNESS

13. Negation of the Three States of Experience ... 57
14. Mind as Witness ... 61
15. Where the Mind becomes No-mind ... 65
16. Witness is the Self - our true identity ... 67

Part V
SELF AS WORLD

17. Suffering of Jiva	73
18. The Cause and Remedy of Suffering	77
19. Non-dual Self as the World	83
20. Vision of Sameness	87

Part VI
YOGA

21. Controlling the Mind	93
22. Restraint of Mind using Self-Knowledge	97
23. Meditation on Ishvara	101
24. Readiness of the Mind	107
25. Discrimination and Detachment	111
26. Obstacles of the Mind	115
27. Asparsa Yoga	119
28. The Self and Empirical Experiences	123

Part VII
ATMAN

29. Identification with Unreal and Seeing the non-dual Reality	131
30. Non-Origination	137
31. Falsifying Owner of Cognition	143
32. The Empirical and Ultimate Truth	147
33. Arising of Fullness	151
About the Author	153

FOREWORD

The author has been a family friend for many years. He is a retired Information Technology professional. He has been a devoted student of Vedantic scriptures since an early age. His parents and other family members inculcated in him the quest for being a good human being, which eventually led him to seek the knowledge of Self through the use of Vedantic texts. He has a wealth of knowledge about different aspects of Vedanta, and conversing with him is always educating as he generously shares what he knows, and it is inspiring. One thing that was remarkable about the author is his priority and continuous focus on the scriptural studies. He not only focuses on his own spiritual development but continues to take a keen interest in friends and family members to increase their affinity toward the scriptures starting from youth to seniors.

Everyone is seeking to be happy and secure. With our senses being naturally directed outward, we seek happiness outside, in objects, possessions, relations, etc. When we achieve what we desire, we become happy. When we achieve what we think gives us security, we feel secure. Our state of mind quickly changes the moment we realize that there is something else out there that would make us happier, more secure! Is there an end to this? Do we even know this is what is going on in our life? We keep running for one thing after another! Have we ever looked at our own life to recognize this constant triumph to be happy and secure? The moment we learn about something better, bigger out there, we feel that we need that to feel happier and more secure! If we are alert enough, we realize that we do not have lasting happiness and security.

In this day and age of smart gadgets and social media, when we are constantly bombarded with information from outside, and we habitually become constantly attentive to that information, it is becoming more difficult to find quiet time with oneself to introspect. However, we know we want lasting happiness, and at times we feel we want to be free from this constant struggle to achieve that. If so, we ought to do some deeper analysis of life. As we look at our experiences in life, we see that whatever we experience changes. Whatever has been created (objects, relations, etc.) changes and perishes eventually. However, there is something that is there at all times to witness what is going on. What is that? What is its real nature? Does that change with experiences, or is it changeless?

To answer these and other such questions, Vedant uses several different methods (*prakriyas*). One of them is *Avastha-traya prakriya*. *Mandukya Upanishad* and *Mandukya Karika* are some of the most important texts of Vedanta that use this method that the author has referred to in this book. Everyone has three states of experience - waking, dream, and deep sleep. This book decodes these three states in-depth and takes us face to face with our immortal self, which is *ever free from suffering, fearless*, and *peaceful*. With its unique *rational and experiential* approach, it takes us on a journey that would help us understand who we truly are. It describes the human mind, the role of it in piercing the human experience. It also points out the obstacles that the mind can come across and how Yoga can help us remove those obstacles. Meditation methods are also explained that would be a tremendous help in purifying the mind to reach the goal of understanding the experiences and reaching the self. This book gets us out of our mundane routine, makes us think about the life that is fleeting, and provides insight into the truth of our experiences.

I hope the readers find this book meaningful and impactful. I wish the readers the best to be graced for their continued interest in such subjects as shared in this book.

Sujata Dave, PMP

Texas

PREFACE

As human beings, we are gifted with self-consciousness. It makes us ask what is the purpose and the ultimate goal of human life? Our ability to query and reach the truth of our own existence as human beings is an exceptional capacity awarded only to human beings in the creation. No thinking person will say, I just want to live life, and do not want to think about the ultimate truth of human life and the universe. If we show negligence and avoidance to the most crucial query of our life, then we insult our own intellect and self-consciousness. We need to admit first our ignorance about the truth of life, and use the gifted capacity of inquiring into the truth to remove the ignorance of life.

The life of a human being means experiences. We go through different experiences, starting with our birth as an ignorant child, growing as an educated adult, being an accomplished middle-aged person, experiencing the helplessness of old age, and finally ending with death. Nay. Death is also an experience. We can see that our life means the sum of all experiences that we go through. All experiences include pleasant as well as unpleasant experiences. We tend to welcome experiences that make us happy and to avoid or disdain experiences that we distaste. We all want perfect undying happiness and security as a result of these experiences. Should we wait for the pleasurable experiences to come, and try to avoid unwanted experiences as much as possible? How much we try, we can't eliminate the unwanted experiences of our life and perfect our experiences at the level where we become totally satisfied and secure. Our repetition of effort to perfect our situation and experiences shows that they can become better, but not perfect up to the level we want. We all are struggling for absolute freedom, happiness, and immortality, *ultimately* as our human goal. Few of us directly realize this; others are working indirectly, not yet knowing that I want lasting peace and happiness, no death and sorrow, and fearlessness.

Like a tiger trapped in a cage, a human is bound by experiences of pain and pleasure. All experiences are perishable. Even after going to paradise, we have to return once the merits of our actions are exhausted. Then, what to say about the perishability of the results of actions here. Should we want to remain in the cage and eat what is given by experience as a result of our action, or break forth the cage of experience and become free? We are always affected by our experiences and become happy and sad. One day, we need to wake up from enjoying the fruits of our *Karma*, various experiences, and ask, what is the truth of the human experience? The promise of freedom that we want lies in understanding our *experience in depth*.

Once we, as a self-conscious human being, recognize our limitations and understand that our relatively happy situation is subject to suffering and sorrow, we will start looking for the cure of the disease of *Samsara*. Is there a place that is free from desire, fear, and grief? Is there a place where permanent effortless objectless happiness and peace reside? The suffering and sorrow are our constant companions. As human beings, we are subject to *Samsara* or birth, death, and sorrow. Where is the solution of desire, fear, anger, death, birth, grief, and sadness? We do not need the temporary painkiller solution, but a permanent solution for the evils of our human existence.

The decision to pursue a spiritual life can come after sufficiently discriminating, analyzing human life and its experiences. Spiritual life is not shying away from the secular life of a human being, but to enhance it, take it to its final destination, and its *ultimate well-being*. Vedant is a complete analysis of the human experience. It clearly shows what is generally missed by a human being that is of the highest importance in solving the riddle of *Samsara*. Vedant starts from what we experience as the world and goes deeper and deeper until the unifying thread of our experiences is reached.

The beauty of Vedant is the use of a human being's highest gifted rational faculty of *buddhi* or intellect to enhance the quality of human life to its ultimate destination of well-being known as *Param Padam*. The effort of *Moksha* or liberation means recovering to or *situating in one's own true nature*, rather than going somewhere from wherever one is or experiencing something new, which is not experienced until now. *Moksha* means to us, that by finding out the real nature of the individual, we can conquer the highest battle of human life and get absolute happiness and immortality.

The question is, what is my real identity? Such questions become vital to us to a discriminating person. Which one is my real identity, when I am awake, or when I am dreaming? Where do I go in the night? From where do I come out in the morning? What is the truth about the objects, including the different beings that I see and interact with, while I am awake and when I am dreaming? Can these objects, including beings, cause unhappiness or happiness to me? Is the deep sleep experience the most exalted? Is the happiness experienced during deep sleep the highest? Where do my desires originate? What is this unconscious force in my experience that impels me to act against my conscious will, and changes my conscious behaviors? What is my relationship with the other living beings and inanimate objects? Is the world separate and independent of me? Are there as many shelves as there are bodies? Is there a relationship between when I am awake and when I am dreaming? Is there a relationship between when I am awake or dreaming, and when I am sleeping? When I am awake or dreaming, I am happy without any worries, but I become sad sometimes.

Should I always try to forget the worries of the world by taking sleeping pills? Where are my pain and pleasure-giving experiences stored in miniature form? What is the truth of a sensual experience? From which root are my thoughts, feelings, and perceptions flowing and being controlled? How do my likes and dislikes come into being? Am I an individual self? Am I helpless in experiencing pain and pleasure? What am I, and what makes up the world? Who made me and the world? Can I free myself from the limitations of my mind and body? Where do I go after death? Is there a God in my experience? Can I experience God? What is God like? Is there a unity beneath the human experience? Can I combine all experiences and reach the unity underlying it? Can that unity make my life better?

These are all critical questions of each human being, and it comes with our existence as a human being. In order to find answers to the above question that every human has or will have, we need to *pierce the human* experience in the light of

Vedant as guided by Vedant. The process of self-knowledge shown by Vedant is nothing but coming out of the self-created turmoil of psychological and physiological processes with an explicit knowledge of their essence. The highest effort an individual person can do is to liberate himself from the limitation of individuality, and bonds of ignorance, desire, and action - *Aham Yagna*. After the effort of *Moksha* using the path of knowledge, nothing else is left for a human being to do, know, and desire.

By inquiring and applying discrimination based on three states of waking, dream, and deep sleep, Vedant step by step elevates us to the unifying knowledge of non-dual self of pure awareness. We will make this journey experientially as well as intellectually. We can make this journey by rigorous analysis of three states of human experience and correcting all our errors in thinking. We can consider all possible options and refute the wrong conclusion. The Vedant shows that non-dual consciousness is the *self of duality*.

If all our experiences are of the same essence of the non-dual Self, then by recognizing the non-dual self, we know the total human experience. In the same way, when we see gold as a substance, then we know a gold ring, necklace, etc., all we know at once. The innermost non-dual Self of a human being is the truth of all experience. All experiences finally become unified in their non-dual essence, which is the self of us.

The Vedant asks us how the immortal, fearless, non-dual, and peaceful self becomes a mortal, dual, suffering, and fearful individual or *Jiva*? The Vedant asks us how the birthless and self-revealing becomes born, and ignorant Jiva?

When going through this journey of ours from an individual to the unborn self, we will frequently refer to **Mandukya Upanishad**, abbreviated as **M.U** and **Mandukya Karika**, abbreviated as **M.K**. I kept these most critical texts of Vedant as a reference for decoding our experience.

When solving the puzzle game, we combine all individual pieces of the puzzle, put them together, and we see the full picture. In the same way, for solving the riddle of human experience, we need to consider each and every human experience as an individual piece, then combine them to generate unifying knowledge and discover the full person.

The initial chapters of the book find the need for piercing human experience and discover that it is, in fact, our identity that we are searching for. It also points out the limitations of human life without understanding the human experience. It describes the method of decoding the human experience.

The following chapters of the book start examining the human experience beginning with the physical world made up of objects. It discovers the physical identity of ours. Then, it proceeds its inquiry to the world of subtle objects. It uncovers the mind as our real identity. It is using the learnings of waking and dream state experiences to arrive at its conclusion. Also, it compares the dream and waking state experiences.

Next, the book looks into the most forgotten realm of the human experience, the kingdom of deep sleep. It finds out its significance and relation to the other states of human experience. Concluding the deep sleep experience, we find out that God or *Ishvara* is our real identity.

Most of us stop here in terms of human experience. The next few chapters of the book discover the most important findings about human being's real identity. The real identity of the human being or self is the *experience of experience* or non-dual experience, the sum total of all our experiences. It clearly defines the method of investigation to arrive at the conclusion of the *non-dual self* as the *reality of the universe*.

The following couple of chapters delineates the implication of the non-dual knowledge of our real identity and how this knowledge is useful to us. It finds out the cause of human suffering and prescribes the unfailing remedy of it. It describes in detail how we and the world benefit from this knowledge. How non-dual knowledge is a blessing to humanity irrespective of the differences of the skin, color, race, country, sect, religion, and gender. The significant implication of non-dual knowledge is the achievement of a happy human-human and human-environment relationship.

It is the mind that discovers itself. The *Yoga* part of the book describes the *Yoga* or methods of controlling the mind to subdue, discipline, and make it a useful instrument to be able to gain the knowledge of human experience. It finds out the obstacles in the way of the mind, which obstructs our vision. The chapters of the book delineate the methods in detail to remove the barriers in the path of self-knowledge to make our journey easier and happy.

The ending chapters seek and find out the cause of the compulsive force of mind and means to rectify it. What is the *relation of self with empirical experiences*? It examines the cause and effect relation in detail to discover the fact of non-origination. Finally, it includes the contemplations of the ultimate reality.

ACKNOWLEDGMENTS

My parents, *Mahendrabhai* & *Kokilaben*, built in me the goal of being a good, virtuous human being, and they gave me the aim of spirituality. The Importance of moral values, education, and character was their gift to create a good human being out of me. My grandparents always used to take me to nearby temples in our town on foot, and we used to do Darshan of *Shrinathji*, our deity. I did not know that, unconsciously, these gifts built love and respect for *Ishvara* in my heart, which would result in my quest for reality using *Vedant* in later years. My beloved younger sister, *Rajeshwari*, always accompanied me to all my activities even today. I cannot repay the debt to my grandparents, parents, and sister, even if I try many lives.

My first introduction to *Bhagavad Gita* occurred in primary school, where Mother Gita was in the center of the hall. Since then, the *Bhagavad Gita* has kept the place of my spiritual mother. The school principal, *Gitaben*, was very generous and loving to me, and she always inspired me to live a spiritual and disciplined life.

I am indebted to My mother's cousin brother, *Gopalbhai Chokshi*, or *Gopalmama* (Vadodara), who had concretized a spiritual goal in my life. I can say that he had initiated me on the path of spirituality when I was very young. I cannot forget him throughout my life. All the necessary groundwork, such as reading scriptural books, participating in cultural activities, and attending spiritual talks, was regularly performed with him. He introduced me to *Swadhyaya*, which is a spiritual family-based activity of revered and beloved *Shastri Pujya Pandurang Athvale*, who we affectionately call *Dadaji*.

When in college, I was inspired by *Shri Ramkrishna* and *Vivekananda's* works. I frequently visited their centers and studied great characters in-depth, whose influence turned me into a serious seeker of spirituality. The *Swadhyaya activity* gave me the platform that I needed for spiritual and human development ever since I was a child and continuing as a young and intelligent person. *Dadaji* explained all the intricacies of Vedantic philosophy centered on the *Bhagavad Gita*. His simple video lectures are filled with the love of *Ishvara*, and the *Pravachans* are inspiring different *Bhakti* based cultural and spiritual activities. *Dadaji* graced me. When I was very young, *Jitubhai Patel*, *Mahadevbhai Tewar*, and *Gopalmama* personally took care of me about what I used to read, think, and feel. I do not have words to thank *Dadaji* for providing me Ishvara's grace and love as a Guru. I was spiritually nurtured and felt the love of Ishvara, with fellow *swadhyayees*. My head simply bows down to *Dadaji* with gratitude, humility, respect, and love.

The spirituality that was developing in me did not become a concrete experience until I came in touch with the Vedantic lectures of *Swami Dayananda Saraswati* of Arsha Vidya tradition. Even though I was in contact with Shankar bhashya on *Upanishads* since I was in college, I knew something was still lacking in my knowledge and experience. After studying

Shankar bhashya commentaries of Swami Dayananda's tradition, I found the missing link. I found myself dumb here due to the lack of words for the Swamiji. I sat before his samadhi at the Rishikesh ashram and paid respect to him.

I want to acknowledge my gorgeous, caring, and loving wife, *Yamini*; intelligent, dedicated, and lovely son *Atri*; charming, determined, and loving daughter *Charvi*; vigorous, smart, and loving daughter-in-law *Jinal* for their continuous loving support for me. Spirituality cannot grow without loving support from the family. I am grateful to my son, daughter, and the wife for eagerly and continuously supporting me in the direction of spirituality for many years. I want to especially thank *Atri* and *Jinal* for their help in the publication of this book.

I am grateful to *Sujata Dave* for lucidly introducing the topic in the forward, and she and her family's invaluable spiritually nourishing friendship over many years. I am *indebted forever and bow with reverence* to the tradition of *Gaudapadacarya and Adi Shankaracharya*. I do not know how to express my sincere gratitude to all that played a role in developing the non-dual vision of *Vedant* in me, as described in the *Shruti*. Finally, let me acknowledge *Ishvara*, the self of all, with love and respect, and *without whose grace* nothing would have been possible.

PART I
SEARCHING THE SELF

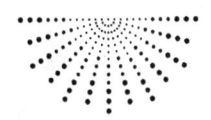

1
NEED FOR PIERCING HUMAN EXPERIENCE

Is there a need for a human being to understand his experience? Here, human experience means the totality of human experience and not the partial human experience. We may say that we do not need to because we are already doing that. As a mature self-conscious human being, we are not only experiencing but also judging our experiences. Yes, but an individual mind that interprets human experiences differs from one individual to another, and hence conclusions that are derived are different even in the same situations or experiences. We do understand our experience because a human being is gifted with the precious cognitive faculty of intellect. Still, most often, we take our experiences at their *face value* or practical value, rather than knowing our experience to its *maximum depth*.

As human beings, our life activities, desires, relationships, feelings, and thinking are driven by the urge of fullness, immortality, and security. Every human being is a river flowing towards the ocean. Every life or being without exception is seeking total fulfillment and freedom. Every human being can't rest until he experiences fullness, complete satisfaction, or absolute happiness. Every human being can't rest until he finds total freedom from all limitations. Every human being can't rest until he finds himself as *Ishvara* or lord of the universe. The constant longing of the human being's faculties of reason, emotion, vital, and physical can never be satisfied until they recognize their source – the *self of the human experience*. Spiritually, we can say that the soul can rest only after recognizing his divine or Godly nature. Rationally, we can say that as a human being, one cannot rest until he finds the *self of the universe* or the *self of the totality of all human experiences*.

Shortcomings of human life are mortality, constant seeking and becoming something, sorrow, conflict, a feeling of smallness, and helplessness. Every human being knowingly or unknowingly seeks to find the solution to his insecurity and unhappiness. Human life is nothing but a search for absolute happiness and immortality.

Enjoying objects of the world and pleasures, vacations, position, wealth, health, and transactional relationships are just starting points towards the ocean of fullness and fail to give lasting happiness. However, they provide reflection or bites of joy and freedom. They provide some testimony that happiness and freedom lie somewhere in a human being, which he seeks through all his activities.

When we take our experiences at their *face value* and never know them correctly, our human goal of immortality, happiness, and security will be ever elusive. The reason is that the human intellect is subjected to not knowing or *Avidya* and knows experiences not as they are, but wrongly. As a result, our experience of suffering, fear, and grief can never leave us. As a human being, we are subjected to "I enjoy," then "I suffer" states of suffering or *Samsara* because of *Avidya* or misinterpreting our human experiences. We suffer from mental and bodily complexes like, "I am alone," " I am depressed," " I hate the world," "I hate myself," " I am sad," "I am fearful," " I am aged", etc. We suffer from an endless modification of our bodily and mental health daily. Still, we do not understand that the cause of suffering or *Samsara* does not lie outside of us, but in the *self-ignorance* or not knowing, and not unifying our experiences through *self-knowledge*. We are *what we know*. If our cognition of intellect develops in seeing *non-dual* unity in the variety of experiences, then we can win our human battle of desire, fear, sorrow, worries, and mortality.

Self-knowledge is the developed or cultivated knowledge through inquiry into the human experience, considering it as raw data to be examined. Developing *self-knowledge* in the intellect is to use Vedantic reasoning as a light to guide our inquiry into the nature of human experience. The peculiarity of *Vedant* is that it is based on human reason and stretches the human reason until the self or unity of our experiences is discovered or recognized. Wrongly seeing our human experience creates suffering for us and keeps us bound to *Samsara*, while seeing the truth of the totality of human experience frees us from the bonds of *Samsara*. *Self-ignorance* is the cause of our suffering, and hence its antithesis, *self-knowledge* is the cure for it.

We know how the child looks at his experiences. After growing up, we do not rejoice in toys as we used to do when we were children. But as an average adult self-conscious personality, we also suffer from strong attachment and aversion. We generally find the cause of our suffering outside of us in the world and rest our effort of intellect. Other times, we say that "I am like this or that and cannot change," and rest our effort of mind by making a human being a slave of happenings.

If we can find unity underlying our own experiences, then we can achieve what we always want. The goal of human life is *fearlessness* or deathlessness and happiness or *freedom from sorrow*. If we understand our experiences from the height of this unity of self, then all varieties of experiences cannot affect us.

The human experience has a form like, " I see the mango tree," " I hear this song," "I am sad today," " I am overjoyed," "I like this," "I do not like this", etc. Human experience consists of the experiencer, experience, and the means of experience. Let us see if there is a self or unity behind our variegated experiences. *Piercing human experience* means finding this *non-dual* unity in the guise of diverse, manifold, and essentially dualistic human experiences. If taken at *face value*, human experience seems individual, ephemeral and made of separate entities. When we look at our experience closely with the help of Vedant or *Shruti*, we start seeing something always constant, pervasive, knowing, universal, and an essential element in the human experience. We call that unchanging, essential, and the "knowing" element of human experience as the *self of experience*. We need to pay attention to that element of experience, which unifies innumerable varied experiences into one *indivisible whole*. The *Bhagavad Gita*[1] beautifully expresses that it is the limitless and changeless self that enters and sustains the three worlds (experience).

We do understand the need to cut through the human experience with the sword of *self-knowledge* obtained through Vedant or *Shruti*. *Chandogya Upanishad*[2] says that the *knower of the self crosses sorrow*. Let us untangle the human experience at its greatest depth and free the human self from sorrow, desire, and fear. As a result, a human can appreciate and really enjoy the present life in the midst of whatever experiences are presented to him by his past deeds.

---

1. 15.17
2. 1.3.1

2
DEFINING THE MIND

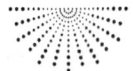

Before we start analyzing our experiences, we need to define a few standard terms. To analyze the experience, we need to pay attention to the instrument of experience. It is the mind through which we gather our experiences. Our mind is the instrument of experience. Let us describe some common terms for our use in understanding our experiences.

Mind by nature is a continuous stream of thoughts. Like a film screen, frames of desires, emotions, sensations, and perceptions of taste, hearing, touch, sight, and smell are continuously flowing in the mind. The mind is always in the state of flux. The mind, like a skilled actor, rapidly *assumes various forms*. The mind always keeps modifying itself into one form of thought to another. Continuous change is the nature of the mind. The *Bhagavad Gita*[1] declares that by nature, the mind is momentary and fickle. The mind is conceiving, imagining, or conceptualizing processes, which assumes different forms. We need to consider these mental functions of memory, thinking alternatives, feelings, decision making, and volition as the mind when we try to understand our experience. The

Buddhi or intellect is reasoning, volition, and ascertaining *the real nature of things* capacity, which is called the higher mind. The mind is called the inner instrument of experience.

Senses are five perceptions of the external mind. Senses form an outer instrument of experience in the form of hearing, seeing, tasting, smelling, and touching. Senses have corresponding objects in the external world like hearing has sound, seeing has form, etc. Senses gathers information about the external world and provides it to the inner instrument of experience for analysis.

Ego is a sense of agency of doing and enjoying. The individual self or *Jiva* is one who eats the fruits of his actions. Ego is *Aham Pratyay*, who appears in the various roles of a feeler, thinker, enjoyer, smeller, tester, etc. Ego is the idea of ownership of the instrument of knowing, *Pramata*. "I do," "I know," and "I enjoy" are the primary expressions of the ego-sense.

The Mind and senses are *Praman* or instruments of the knowledge. One who has ownership of this inner and outer instrument of experience is called *Pramata*, a sense of agency idea or ego.

Collectively, ego, inner and outer instruments of experience all are *changing mind* or *Vrittis*. Hence let us call them collectively the mind only for our analysis. We will use the word consciousness or *Chaitanya* or *Atman* for the self, and not for the mind.

---

1. 6.26

3
DISCRIMINATING BETWEEN REAL AND UNREAL

*E*very human being needs to discover and recognize himself as *Satchitananda* or *Ishvara*. A human being is endowed with the intellect or *Buddhi*. The power of thinking and discrimination needs to be developed to arrive at what 'I am,' or what *my identity* really is. Since the power of knowledge is concerned with the *real nature of things*, it can discriminate reality or 'what is' from falsehood or 'what is not.' *Buddhi* can dive into the darkness of ignorance and arrive at a conclusion about the reality of things.

Atma-anatman Viveka is discerning what stays or *Nitya* and what is fleeting or *Anitya* in a *human being's experience*. We need to analyze our experiences in the light of Vedant or *Shruti* and develop the power of discrimination to be able to distinguish *self* from *non-self* and its *Svarupa* or real nature.

The *Bhagavad Gita*[1] says to a man to cut self-doubt and self-ignorance asunder by developing thinking and discrimination about *self* and *non-self*. If I know that I am the non-dual, whole self, then differences in mind, body, and personality between you and me will vanish. If used in the direction of discrimination of three states, *Buddhi* can lead us to the ultimate realization that "I am" is the essence of the whole universe of names and forms.

If I know that I am the knowledge itself or *Chit svarupa*, then what further knowledge should I seek? *Shvetashvatara Upanishad*[2] declares that man's sorrow comes to an end without knowing the self only if he can roll up the sky. In other words, it is impossible to end the sorrow and misery of a human being without acquiring the knowledge of the self or *true identity* of a human being.

Self-discrimination leads to the essence of our being by removing a mix in of non-essential parts of our experience. The knower and known are two parts mixed up in our experience. We need to separate the knower from the known carefully, and then our *Buddhi* can realize that the known is not essentially separate from the knower. In other words, known is nothing but the knower *in its essence*. Knowledge derived out of *discrimination based on one's own experiences* will be final and will not diminish in any case. Removed doubt and ignorance through discrimination will never come back. All objective experiences come and go away, even if it is a trance or *samadhi* experience. On the other hand, the knowledge of the self, which is derived out of discrimination, does not go away because it is about the eternal self. Discrimination and inquiry that one can do about the self and non-self is the boat that carries one to the other shore of *Samsara*. *Bhagavad Gita*[3] declares that we can break the bondage of actions using the discrimination between real and unreal.

We are not looking for some yet to come in the future, objective experience of the mind. But our goal is to turn to the self, which is manifesting as all objective experiences - *Anubhuti svarupa*. *Buddhi* or human intellect is equipped with the ability to cognize the real nature of things. We need to use this ability of the human mind to aim or turn towards the fundamental nature of the self. This ability of *Buddhi* is used in Vedant to inquire about the real nature of the self.

Another ability of the mind is to meditate without aiming at the real nature of the self. This ability is a mental action without the goal of cognizing the real nature of a thing. For example, if I meditate on God and keep thinking that I am God or like a God. In this case, I already know that I am such-and-such, and I am trying to superimpose God on me. The ability of the mind to meditate without aiming at the real nature of the self can help only a dispersed mind to become one-pointed and gathered, but not useful at a later stage where the real nature of the self needs to be discovered.

Maya is a *seemingly* real phenomenon. Maya becomes fact in experience if we do not bother to discriminate between what is real and what appears to be. For this reason, different minds interpret the same reality, entirely different from what it is. Upon discrimination, whatever is unreal will vanish in the wake of knowledge of *Buddhi*. In our experience, facts and appearances are mixed up. This is the primary purpose of distinguishing the facts from the beliefs of our experience. Due to *Maya* or *Avidya*, different minds or people follow different goals, activities, desires, feelings, and thoughts.

We will be primarily using the Vedantic reason to churn three states of experience of a human being and arrive at the conclusion that does not benefit only us but to a great extent the whole world.

---

1. 4.42
2. 6.20
3. 2.39

4
SEARCHING THE SELF OF THE HUMAN BEING

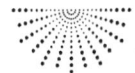

As a human being, our total experience consists of three states of waking, dream, and deep sleep. Besides these categories of experience, we know nothing. We need to include the whole of our experience and find the self of it. If we can realize the unity of self behind this whole human experience, then the experience will make sense to us as well as we can make ourselves free from the bonds of experience. We can free ourselves from the bond of the unwanted experience of pleasure and pain called *Samsara* only when we know ourselves as the *self of the experience*. It is not that unexpected and undesirable experiences do not happen after realizing the self of three states, but the truth is that one remains unaffected while facing them.

Understanding the human experience in depth is the same as finding a human being's *self* or *essential nature* or *real identity*. We need to dig into these waking, dream, and deep sleep states, one by one and analyze it properly. Only by *combining the knowledge* derived from all the three states of experience can we realize ourselves as the *Atman* - the self of all. The unifying knowledge is born after applying reason to the three states of our experience, which leads to *immediate liberation*. The application of the Vedantic reasoning on three states finds the common and universal entity of all three states and resolves the differences among the three states. The application of Vedantic reason on the three states of experience makes us *merge* or *resolve* waking state to dream state, dream state to deep sleep, and ultimately to the *stateless self* of all states. With the *unified knowledge* generated, we can discover the true identity of a human being. This recognition of our *self of experience terminates our search of self* and gives us the ultimate peace and security.

Most of our experiences are in the form of " I know the object." Our experiences consist of two essential parts. The knower and the known. The experiencer and experienced. The seer and seen. We need to dig into what is being experienced to arrive at the nature of the known. Then, what about the knower? What is the nature of the knower, is the knower knowable? How is the knower related to known? Is there any relation to what we see with the one *who sees* it? We need to see if there is any relation between experienced phenomena and the experiencer of the phenomena. Is our experience dual or non-dual or both? We need to answer all these questions.

We will refer to our data of experience, which we always have, and look at them in the light of Vedantic reason and scrutiny of our intellect. After all, reason is the highest faculty awarded to a human being.

Our search of self will proceed in this way, both experientially and rationally. This approach is the only way to solve the riddle of human life because it takes every single experience into account and applies the intellect to it as guided by Vedant.

The known part of our experience changes and modifies continuously, but the knower part remains the same. It gives us the clue of searching ourselves as the knower of experience where experience changes and is temporary, but we as knower remains there, as it is without changing. Our ability to recall our experiences and analyze our experiences using reason is the most excellent tool awarded to us. It enables us to come out of the *maze of experiences* and make every experience meaningful and beneficial to us and all beings.

Generally, the knower and known is too mixed up in our experience, and we do not recognize them separately. We need to carefully separate them because their nature is different from each other, and later resolve the known into the knower. *Bhagavad Gita*[1] mentions clearly that the knowledge of the known and the knower is the right knowledge. In other words, this knowledge becomes the *means of liberation* for a human being. Knowing that the real self of a human being is in the form of three states of universal experience, every experience becomes liberating and reveals the self.

---

1. 13.2

PART II
WORLD AS OBJECTS

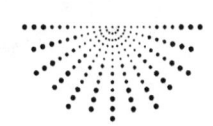

5
WAKING STATE - WORLD AS PHYSICAL OBJECTS

*L*et us start by looking into our experience of *waking state*. Let us describe our experience of waking state.

As soon as we wake up after sleep, we encounter another entity called the world. We recognize that we are separate from this entity called the world, and the world is *separate and independent* from us. We start interacting with the world. We see that the world is made up of a myriad of physical objects, including beings, like humans, animals, plants, planets, stones, etc. We see a world consists of objects made up of matter. Not only that, but we also recognize that each object has an independent existence and that they are very real, as real as we are real. In other words, each object has bytes of existence and exists in their own right. When we say "I saw a tree," it means that I see an entity called a tree with its unique, peculiar qualities that define its treeness, as distinguished from the rest of the objects. Each object we see in the waking state is independent and separate from each other. We see other human beings like us, but as separately existing and unique. We see and experience a world made up of *gross objects*, including *beings*.

In our waking state experience, who sees or experiences these objects? It is us. As an individual, we are endowed with a waking state personality made up of physical body and mind. I consider myself an individual or *Jiva* in the waking state, whose identity is based on the *mind and physical body*. I am a mind-body complex based identity, who is the *waker* in the waking state. We see ourselves as tied with the complex of a specific body and mind that imparts to us our unique identity in the waking state. We describe ourselves as "I am six feet tall," "I am a woman," "I am a man," " I am white," " I am black," "I am a doctor," "I am a lawyer," "I am lonely," "I am sad," "I am virtuous," etc. The personality is our waking state identity based on attributes of thoughts, feelings, and sensations. We introduce ourselves as such and such, coming from this family, country, race, religion, etc.

As *Jivas* or individuals, we have doership and enjoyership. We earn through work and enjoy the results of our work. We achieve money, status, family, power, and enjoy them. To enjoy, we achieve what we want to enjoy in life. The description of our waking state personality is "I know," "I do," and "I enjoy." Furthermore, I am a responsible person and aware of my rights. As a *waker*, I am *Pramata* or knower of the world who *owns* the inner instrument or mind, senses, and body.

We enjoy and suffer. We become peaceful and suddenly angry. We are vulnerable to feelings, thoughts, sensations, memory, and desires as a *waker ego*. We are haunted by the fear of death, a sense of lack, i.e., desire, and helplessness as *Jiva*. We can't avoid the desire or incompleteness, fear, grief, and sorrow in our *waking self*. We can't prevent the suffering of pain and pleasure, attachment and aversion, death, and disease in our waking state experience.

In our experience of waking state, we are *conscious of the external world* and ourselves as two real *separate entities* interacting with each other. M.U.[1] describes the waking state experience as *Bahis Pragna* because we have "consciousness of external or other than me." We are aware of the outward universe due to the *outward nature of the senses*. In the waking state, we are aware of *external physical objects* which are *real*, having their own reality or existence. The M.K.[2] represents this waker self as *Vishva*. In the waking state, we are the enjoyer or experiencer of the gross physical objects, *"Stuhl Bhuk."*

Our waking state body is composed of five elements of space, air, fire, water, and earth. We have five senses of knowledge situated as eye (vision), ear (hearing), nose (smell), tongue (taste) and skin (touch). For example, when we say "I saw a flower," our eye grasps the color and shape of a flower. Then we smell it and discover it is the rose. The flower gives stimuli to our eye, nose, then it picks up that sense of vibration and sends it to the mind. The mind collates the sense impressions, takes the form of *rose thought*, and then the intellect decides that object as the rose. In other words, the senses, the inner instrument of the mind, and the intellect must work together and certify that as the knowledge of the rose.

So, the knower (*Pramata*), the instrument of knowledge (*Pramana*), and the known (*Prameya*) are different in the waking state. Every object of the external world has to prove itself through our sensory organs and mind to exist as objects in their own right.

---

1. 1.3
2. 1.1

6
DREAM STATE - WORLD AS SUBTLE OBJECTS

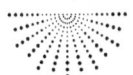

*L*et us look at our dream state experiences. Generally, we discard this state of experience, considering it as unreal and not bearing much weight compared to our waking state experience. However, in Vedanta, the dream state is regarded as even more important than waking, to learn about ultimate reality and search for our complete self. Let us describe our dream state experience.

As soon as we wake up in the dream state, we encounter a separate entity called the world made up of subtle objects. We recognize that we are separate from this entity called the world, and the world is *separate and independent* from us. We start interacting with the world. We see that the world is made up of a myriad of subtle objects, including beings, that do not actually exist, such as humans, animals, plants, planets, stones, etc. We see a world consisting of objects made up of subtle matter or thought. Not only that, but we also recognize that each object has an independent existence and that they are quite real as we are. We do not see physically real gross objects, but we do see *object appearances* made up of thought or mind. We feel objects appear and disappear quickly and are not stable.

In our dream state experience, who sees or experiences these objects? It is us. As an individual, we are endowed with a dream state personality made up of *subtle* body and mind. I consider myself an individual or *Jiva* in the dream state, whose identity is based on the mind and subtle body. I am a subtle mind-body complex based identity, who is the dreamer in the dream state.

In the dream state, the *subject* is us, the *object* is the world, and their relationship is still intact, and hence, we still suffer from *pain* and *pleasure*. We still suffer from all complexes and desires of an individual, the same as the waking state. Our individual problems still remain in the dream state but related to our dream state personality. We enjoy and suffer. We become peaceful and suddenly angry. We are vulnerable to feelings, thoughts, sensations, memory, and desires as a *dreamer ego*. We are haunted by the fear of death, a sense of lack, i.e., desire, and helplessness as *Jiva*. We can't avoid the desire or incompleteness, fear, grief, and sorrow in our *dreamer self*. We can't prevent the suffering of pain and pleasure, attachment and aversion, death, and disease in our dream state experience.

Although, in our dream state of experience, we do not identify with the *gross physical senses and body*. Our experiences are *made up of mind* only. Dream state cars, people, myself, animals, mountains, trees, etc. are nothing but *made up of thoughts*. It is the mind playing within itself. The M.U.[1] describes the experience of the dream state succinctly as *Antah Pragna* or *consciousness of internal objects*. In a dream state, we are *inwardly conscious*; everything is seen within. It is the mind playing all roles. It is described as *Taijas* or the self, which is made up of light of mind which experiences the dream state. The mind is considered as internal compared to the outward nature of the senses. Even though there are no real physical objects, we still see objects made up of thoughts of the mind. We enjoy or experience the subtle objects created by *impressions stored in mind* or *Vasanas*. Our mind impresses itself with the waking state experiences and reproduces them in the dream state.

We experience everything within our bodies only. In other words, our body is lying in bed and does not go out to experience the other country that we visited in the dream. Dream experience is local and confined to the body. Another example is that we are having dinner with friends in a small restaurant far away from home. Suddenly, when we wake up, we do not find friends or a small restaurant, but we find ourselves in the bed. Hence, we understand that dream experiences are localized and confined to the body only.

---

1. 1.4

PART III
OBJECTS AS MIND

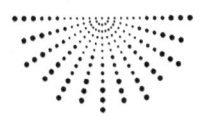

7
LEARNING FROM DREAM STATE

We, again and again, go through dream state and waking state experiences every day and night. We avoid dream state experiences as not useful or unreal and confine our identity as *waker* only. As a result, we never analyze dream state experiences from the *reality perspective*. Hence, our investigation into the real nature of the world does not go any further, and we are stuck with waking state issues. Let us analyze the dream state experiences after waking up.

After waking up, what do I realize? Let us divide the dream state experience into dreamer (*Swapna Drik*), dreamer's mind (*Swapna Drik Chitta*), and whatever is seen (*Swapna Drik Chitta Drishya*) in the dream. I realize that whatever I saw or experienced in the dream was nothing but *my mind only*. What I was considering real when I was dreaming, upon waking up, proved to be *unreal* or an *appearance of my mind*. All bad or good dream content, whatever I saw like friends, enemies, dogs, relatives, trees, mountains, houses, countries, people, insects, etc., was in my mind, *non-separate* from my mind, and hence *myself alone*. The entire dream content was in fact, my mind imagining and thinking. All dream objects, including my running around in the dream, were nothing but my mind's activities. *All that is seen is unreal* or not having its *own substance*, but is activities of the dreamer's mind. Just like a golden ring cannot exist apart from the gold; similarly, all objects, including *Jivas*, seen in the dream cannot exist apart from the dreamer's mind. All, whether external or internal objects are nothing but mind only. No *causal relation* exists between the mind and its objects.

When we want to discover the reality and unity behind the three states of human experience, we need to analyze the experiences of all the states from the *reality perspective*. From the dream state, we can conclude that whatever is being seen was nothing but the *seer's mind*. Again, seer's mind is *seer only*. In other words, whatever is of the nature of being perceived is, *in reality*, non-separate from the perceiver. It is the dreamer's mind that appears in the *dual form* of *perceiver* and *perceived*. M.K.[1] declares this truth that the dream content is nothing but the dreamer's mind. The dreamer's mind is not separate from the dreamer himself. We saw a clear division of myself and not-myself or subject and object in the dream, but upon waking up, that duality of subject-object proved unreal and mere *appearance of the mind*. The ego and non-ego division of the dream was illusory and dual form was taken by the dreamer's mind only. Whatever appears as *outside* or external to the dream personality or character is really *inside* the dreamer's mind only.

If we analyze our dream content properly, we see that the dreamer's mind and whatever is seen are not two independent and separate realities, but relative, and depend on each other for their mutual existence. The dreamer's mind and whatever is seen by the dreamer's mind - we cannot think of one without referring to the other. In other words, a perceiver cannot be thought independent of the idea of the perceived. The perceiver and perceived are made of one substance called the dreamer's mind. Dream state experience teaches that whatever was perceived is unreal and essentially non-different than the dreamer. In short, the non-dual mind appeared as dual in the dream state.

---

1. 4.64

8
WAKING AND DREAM STATE ARE THE SAME

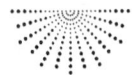

To discover unity behind the waking and dream state, we should not stop here, but extend our learning of the dream state to the waking state. Because the waking experience also is a part of our whole experience, and hence, this wholeness or oneness must have unity behind it. To generate unifying knowledge of both waking and dream phenomena, we should apply the learning of the dream state to the waking state. Our goal is to discover the unity and real nature or identity of the *self of experience*. If any commonality is found between dream and waking state, then we can apply the learning and resolve the differences of these states, and unifying knowledge can be born.

If we analyze the waking state experience based on the learning from the dream state, we discover that from the perspective *of the reality of experience*, the waking state is no different than the dream state. How? Let us look in more detail at the waking state for the unification.

Just like the dream personality has seen dream objects, including other *Jivas*, the waking personality also sees objects, including other *Jivas*. The *subject-object division* is common in both the states as their main characteristic feature. The waking state mind also sees the waking state objects in the same way. The waking state objects have the same character as *being perceived*. Because of this common feature, we can extend our learning of the dream state that whatever is being perceived is unreal and non-different from the seeing mind. It is the same mind in the form of the waking condition taking the *dual form of subject and object*. The objects appear more stable in the waking state than the dream state but are still bound by time and therefore disappear and appear. Common to both the states, objects appear and disappear and are seen by the mind's perceiving nature. The perceiving capacity as a dream or waking perceiver remains the same and never fades away.

In the waking state, we feel that the mind has contacted an object. For example, we saw a flower. Then, our senses get the color and smell of the flower and send its impressions to the mind, and the mind forms an idea of the flower and declares that "It is Jasmine." Here, in this process of perception of the flower, our mind has *never really contacted a real object*. The object flower existed as a *thought* or wave in mind. It is in terms of mind that we perceive, and then we *wrongly infer* that flower as an object exists outside of us. Our intellect attributing existence to the flower is *mere inference* because the mind has never *touched* the real existing object. The M.K.[1] declares that the mind never contacted nor related to the external object. It is the *outward nature of the senses* that makes us believe that the real flower exists outside of us. The external senses pick up the touch, sound, smell, taste, and form.

Objects seen in the waking condition due to its grossness appear more real to us, but in reality, they are similar in nature to the dream condition. Hence, waking state objects are not separate from the waking mind, and the waking mind is waker only.

Looking only from the viewpoint of the waking personality that the world appears as *external and gross objects*. Looking only from the viewpoint of the dream personality that the world appears as *internal and subtle objects*. In the waking state, we identify with the internal mental processes and with external senses. This additional identification of ourselves with the external senses in the waking state makes us believe that the *external world is real and separate* from the mind that sees the external world. In the dream, we see that even though externality and internality is present, objects were nothing but mental activities or thoughts. The same holds true with the waking condition, which is characterized as grosser external objects, but that cannot *give reality to objects*.

During the dream alone, the dream world appears to us as real, and it appears as real as the waking state world. When we are waking, during only that period, the waking world appears to us as real. Each state negates the other—our waking state personality changes when we are dreaming. We may have full dinner in the evening, but in the dream, we may be hungry. Even though we see that the means like food serve an end, like appeasing hunger in the waking state, it is contradicted in the dream state. With this data of experience, M.K.[2] suggests that it is not that the waking state is more real than the dream state or the dream state is more real than the waking state; both *are the same* from the *perspective of reality*.

Dreamer and waker become *one* after the *seen objects* are realized as *not independent of the seeing mind*. The mental activity alone continues. MK.[3] declares that the objects that are not seen in the beginning and the end, but seen only in the middle, are considered *illusory*. Because these objects did not exist in the beginning and are going to disappear in the future, they cannot be said to be real. Hence, objects seen in the waking and dream state both are *equally unreal*.

The external world appears so real to us that we never think about their illusory and mental nature. Our analysis tells us that the external world is not the *cause of the suffering* because it is unreal and not separable from the seeing mind. We strongly think that the external world is a separate and independent reality in itself. This conclusion falls apart when the Vedic reasoning of the dream state is applied to it. How can we consider the external world as our cause of suffering, conflicts, and complaints anymore? The *internality* and *externality* are not two separate entities, but the one non-dual mind *simultaneously* takes the form of both. There is no independent existence of the objective (Adhidaiva) world apart from the subjective (Adhyatmika) world who sees it. The subjective experience is not *caused by* the external world. M.K[4] declares that the *causal relation* of the *external world,* causing pain to the *internal subject,* is assumed because of *ignorance*. Only from the *empirical standpoint,* the outer world causes subjective changes of pain, anger, etc. not from the perspective *of reality*. The suffering of *Jiva* is not due to the external world *causing* it; that is how normally each *Jiva* views it. The cause of suffering does not lie in the external world of objects or persons. The thought process does not attribute existence to the appearing external world after having this knowledge.

The *duality of the subject and object* in the state of waking and dream appears so real because of their *appearance* and the *transactional capacity* or *behaving according to the role*. Although the

WAKING AND DREAM STATE ARE THE SAME

waking and dream world is capable of transaction and appears, it cannot be a reason to give them a *reality of their own*. The reality is not denied, but the reality does not belong to these dualistic states of waking and dream. M.K.[5] gives a fascinating example: the elephant created by a magician appears to us and also conforms to the traits of an elephant, but in reality, it is *naught*. Similarly, it is the non-dual mind working in the form of dualistic states of dream and waking.

What about the ego and body that are experienced in the waking state? Both are unreal because they also become seen. Changes in the body are seen by ourselves as the mind. Hence, the body is imaginary and non-separate from the seeing mind. The ego itself is seen and *not the seer*. Generally, we take ego or waking state personality to be the knower (*Pramata*), but it is not the knower, but the known by the mind. It is the non-dual mind in the waking state also that appears in the dual role of *ego and non-ego*.

The same seeing mind or *self of experience* when identified with the waking condition, sees or experiences the waking world. The same seeing mind or *self of experience* when identified with the dream condition, sees or experiences the dream world. It is the seeing mind that is experiencing both the worlds.

Let us take any object of the world and analyze it. For example, let us take the shirt that I am wearing. Before analysis from the perspective of reality, I see a shirt as reality. When I closely examine the shirt, I find it to be the cloth of which it is made. Now, the shirt is reduced to the cloth, and the cloth becomes the reality of the shirt. I do not see the shirt anymore but see only cloth. I can reduce other shirts also to the cloth. If I examine further, I know the reality of cloth is reduced to fibers of which the cloth is made. Now, I can even reduce all different types of clothes to fibers only, if I continue my analysis, from fiber to what fiber is made up of and even further to atoms and kinetic forces. But ultimately, in the analysis, I see the shirt as a mental concept known to me in mind. This way, we can reduce all the objects to the mental concepts in its ultimate analysis. The static objects are realized as the dynamic cognitive (mental) processes. With the *matter reduced to mind, waking and dream state becomes one.*

---

1. 4.26
2. 2.7
3. 2.6
4. 4.25
5. 4.44

9
IDENTITY AS COMMON MIND

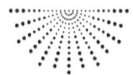

*A*fter reducing all objects as mental concepts, what do we become? How do we feel and think like ourselves?

We feel ourselves or our identity as a universal common but changing cognizing mind. We feel ourselves as thinking and feeling principle as *universal Jiva*. Our identity is one with changing mental functions and not with any objects. We see ourselves as the metaphysical truth of the objects. As a result of our mental cognitive activities, objects appear and disappear. Objects are nothing but reflections of universal mind working. We see our identity is composed of the *changing mind*.

Let us take an analogy to visualize it. Think of an actor playing various roles in a drama. Sometimes, he becomes the cruel king, Ravana. At other times he plays the good king Rama, and yet in some more roles, he plays as a servant, or even a homeless beggar, etc. For the spectators of the dramas, he comes as a different identity in each role he plays. But for him, he sees himself as an actor playing various roles. For himself, he is an identity continuously playing changing roles.

When playing Ravana's role, he sees himself not as Ravana, but an actor skillfully playing the role of Ravan. As an actor, he does *appear as* Ravana, and others see him as Ravana only. For him, Ravana, the king is devoid of reality or concept, and reality is transferred to him, as *an actor playing the role*. Similarly, after analysis of two states of the waking and dream universe, we see ourselves as a common mind, and the external world is reduced to these *changing cognitions* for us. Although, the external word still appears to us in the guise of the objects. We see any other objects, including persons, in terms of these feelings, thinking, sensing, smelling, tasting, hearing, and touching activities of ourselves. The mind is the objectifying and differentiation power, which generates knowledge as its concepts. No knowledge is possible without the *differentiating mind working*.

The incredible thing is, we see ego as nothing but a thought or modification of ourselves or *Aham Vritti* and not an object. Before this analysis, we used to see our identity as this personality or ego on one side and the external world as separate from us. Now, the external world and ego are both *reduced to* specific mental waves of the *universal mind*. M.K.[1] declares that the universal mind first imagines *Jiva*, and then *subjective and objective entities* are *imagined*.

---

1. 2.16

10
CAUSE OF THE WAKING AND DREAM STATE

The question arises: why do we see waking and dream states as different in the first place as we used to see them before analysis? Why does everybody see the waking state as real and the dream state as unreal?

We have already answered this question. Before analyzing these states in the light of Vedantic reason of three states, our different identities, and experiences as the waker and dreamer continues forever. Still, we need to pay more attention to the cause of these states in the first place as it occupies our whole life.

Not knowing the *self of experience* is the cause of seeing these states. Not only are we ignorant about the real nature of the self of experience, but the problem is that we superimpose something else on the self. We superimpose non-self on the self. We assume whatever appears as real and mistake ourselves as body and ego. Because we did not know the real self of experience, it becomes the *basis of the projection* of the waking world and the dream world experiences. The issue is not only of *ignorance* about the reality but compounded by the *error* about the reality. It is the misinterpretation of the reality of experience that we see and experience every day. M.K.[1] declares that *self-delusion* is the cause of the experiences of the waker and dreamer. Again, M.K.[2] states that ignorance of the self is the cause, and the waking state and the dream state is the effect.

The result is suffering, unhappiness, and insecurity that we experience every day. Waves of joy and suffering are tossing us. The fear of mortality inflicts us. We feel so much helplessness and a sense of lack or incompleteness that over the years, we feel life is not worth living.

Every object is fleeting and changing. World objects are appearing and disappearing, and still, we take them as real and permanent. Our body also undergoes many changes such as growth, decomposition, etc., from birth until death. Our ego dies every day in sleep, yet we cling to our ego and love it more than anything else. Over the years of non-investigation into the nature of reality, our ego becomes so stiff that no wisdom can *pour through* us. We feel that we are *born*, *going through experiences* of life, and going to *die* one day. These are all unavoidable outcomes to avoid examining the nature of human experience.

What happens after removing ignorance about the self of experience? It does not mean that waking and dream states do not occur, but it only means that we will not misinterpret the world, ego, and body, as we did before with *ignorance* and *error*.

CAUSE OF THE WAKING AND DREAM STATE

Let us continue our deepening analysis of the human experience because we still need to investigate and analyze the third state of human experience, deep sleep.

---

1. 1.15
2. 1.11, 4.41

11
INACTIVE STATE OF MIND

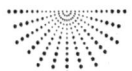

Let us describe our experience of deep Sleep. In Vedant, experiences of all states are equally important to arrive at the whole truth of experience. For further analysis, let us first see what we are experiencing in a deep sleep.

When we come back to a waking state, we describe our deep sleep experience as blissful as, "I enjoyed a restful sleep." We *experience bliss*, which is not dependent on any object. We covet no objects or people in a deep sleep. We are free from desire and sorrow in a deep sleep. We do not experience any other objects in a deep sleep. It is a state of *non-perception* and hence, an *inactive mind*. It is a state of *non-discrimination* or *Avivek*. Therefore, the person is called *sleeping* or *Supta* in the sense of absence of cognitions or mind not working. We are neither aware of ourselves, nor do we know others. No bank account, spouse, children, employment, insurance, problems, etc., exists to be aware of in this state. We do not need to respond to any events, nor do we need to go to work. We are enjoying the state of *no effort*. No worries of anything touches us. We do not comprehend any subtle or gross objects. We experience the deep sleep as the total *absence of objects* and the absence of the *activity of the mind* that perceives it. Like in a dark room, objects lying in the room are not comprehended because of the absence of light. The next day, everything comes back to us as it is.

Brihadaranyaka Upanishad[1] describes the experience of deep sleep as, "where a father becomes not a father, a mother becomes not a mother, worlds no worlds, thief no thief, etc.". We become free from the sorrow and evil of the other two states. In a deep sleep, everything becomes *undifferentiated or unified*. We find no difference between ourselves, other persons, the sun, moon, stars, animals, etc. Nothing is perceived as *separate from us*. Deep sleep is a *non-dual experience*, where the *subject-object duality* of the other two states vanishes. M.U[2] declares the experiencer of this state as the *mass of consciousness or Pragna* and the *enjoyer of bliss* or *Anandbhuk*. M.U says that this state of the mass of *undifferentiated consciousness* is like a gateway leading to experiences of dream and waking states. We neither know the truth nor the untruth in the state of deep sleep. No distinction between subject and object is known.

Our senses, ego, speech, body, and mind get tired because of being engaged in various activities during waking and dream states and want to retire to get full rest. Like a bird comes back to its nest in the night after hunting for food in the daytime. Deep sleep or *Sushupti* is a rejuvenating experience. Our mind, body, ego, senses, and speech become miraculously rejuvenated the next day. As evening approaches, some switch is turned off in us, and every creature wants to go to sleep and forget the world. We sometimes take painkillers as an interim step to fall asleep. When the mind stops in a deep sleep, our problems to confront also disappear with it as well. This way, deep sleep is a negative but blissful experience as we get rid of an effort or *exertion*.

Only our *Prana* or breath continues during sleep. Mind, along with ego, sense, and speech, is absorbed by the *Prana*. Deep sleep or *Sushupti* is a state of temporary death. Deep sleep is a pure causal state compared with dream and waking states. The next day, our mind, along with the ego, the senses, and the speech, emerge just as they were.

---

1. 4.3.22
2. 1.5

12
IDENTITY AS ISHVARA

We sleep every night, then we wake up, then we sleep again, and then we wake up again. It goes on until we die. It never occurs to us that sleep has the most valuable and important message that can enhance and change our life.

What does the *absence of duality and objects* tell us? No objective universe exists in the experience of deep sleep. Deep sleep is an interval in which the knower and known are united. Deep sleep is characterized by not knowing the self or *Avidya*. It is the *seed state of causal ignorance*. The effect of dream and waking state experiences lies *dormant* here. Not knowing the reality or *Avidya* becomes the very cause for *projecting* the *illusory* universe of waking and dream. It is just like how the *not knowing of the rope or substratum* becomes the *cause for the projection of a snake on the rope* in the dark night. This *projecting power* is also called *Vikshepa* in the Vedant.

The state of deep sleep is bound by the cause of *not knowing the reality*. In comparison, the cause and its effect bind the state of dream and waking. The effect is *seeing something else in place of reality*. *Avidya* is thus twofold, *veiling* and *projecting* metaphysical level ignorance, inherent into the intellect of the *Jiva*. *Avidya* continues until the *Jiva* awakens from the *sleep of ignorance* concerning the *self of experience*. This ignorance or *Avidya* cannot remove itself and becomes the cause of *Samsara* or the *suffering of the Jiva*. *Jiva* needs to know the reality of the *self of experience* to awaken from this *seed state of ignorance*.

If we carefully analyze deep sleep, we find that all objects, including beings, disappear here, and also re-emerge from here. M.U.[1] declares the deep sleep state as *Ishvara*, the lord of all, the controller, the inner ruler of all, the knower of all, and the *source* of all. If we really know the deep sleep state, then we can understand the *real nature of the universe*. We realize our real self or *identity as the cause of the universe* - *Ishvara*, the *creator*, *maintainer*, and *destructor* of all. The significance of the non-dual deep sleep state is that it can absorb and recreate the duality over and over again. It is a *measure* of the waking and dream state. As *Ishvara*, we are the resolution point or *laya* of the duality.

Let us combine knowledge generated out of three states. *Active state* and *inactive state* of mind are my *differentiated* and *undifferentiated* aspects. I am the cause of differentiated state or duality and multiplicity of objects. I sometimes exist as an undifferentiated, non-dual state, and then manifest as a dual, differentiated state. When I see duality, I am not in a non-dual state; when I am in a non-dual state, I am not in a dual state. Like in a seed condition, I can't see a tree, and while I am in a tree condition, I can't see the seed. Now, I can see the *causal relationship* between me and the creation.

In other words, there is a tint of ignorance left, which prevents us from seeing our wholeness or undividedness at all times. M.K² declares that traces of seed ignorance characterizes this state. Can we rise above the *causal relation* between us and the creation?

---

1. 6
2. 1.13

PART IV
MIND AS WITNESS

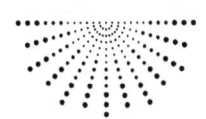

13
NEGATION OF THE THREE STATES OF EXPERIENCE

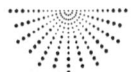

*I*gnorance exists in the state of deep sleep. So far, we have merged the waking state in the dream state, then the dream state in the deep sleep state. We have resolved the *objects* to *concepts*, *concepts* to an active *mind*, and active mind to inactive mind or *causal state of mind*. Our enjoyment progressed from enjoying the gross physical *objects made up of matter*, to the enjoyment of subtle objects made up of the previous *mental impressions*, to the mere *effortless state of bliss*. Our identity or self-knowledge progressed from seeing ourselves as *Vishva* or the whole physical world to the identity of *Taijas* or active and the changing mind and finally to the *Ishvara* or causal self of the universe. It is a significant advance in terms of unifying knowledge resulting from the three states of experiences, but still, a trace of ignorance persists.

We still need to inquire further. But how? We have investigated all that we experience. M.U.[1] gives us the method to reach the ultimate reality from where we stand now. It is by *negating three states* that we can recognize the *ultimate essence of the universe*.

Inquiry cannot proceed anymore into objective states of our experiences but needs to turn to the method of negation to recognize the *substratum of the three states*. Negation of the falsely qualifying attributes that are superimposed on the reality becomes the means to know the ultimate truth. Nothing else is required other than turning on the light to recognize a chair in the darkroom.

For example, to know the truth of rope in the dark, we need to negate the snake, stick, thief, etc. which is superimposed on the rope. The rope as a substrate is not different from a snake, post, thief. Therefore, we cannot see the substrate without negating the covering of the snake, stick, etc., because they are making the rope appear *differently than what it is*.

Thus, the three conditions of *gross, subtle, and seed* qualifying *Atman* are negated or realized as unreal, and other than these three states is *Atman* or the *reality of three states* is indicated. Why? Because the *Atman* or *Brahman* as the underlying substratum of three states is not separate from them. Hence, negating false attributes or *Upadhi* is enough to reveal the *Atman* because the *Atman* is *self-luminous*. Three states appear and disappear in time, while the substratum *Atman* continues and *never appears and disappears*. Reality means that it would have to survive three periods of time. We can verify that, based on our experience, "I am awake, I dreamed, and slept well last night." Here, our identity "I" continued as the same reality, independent of the three states, like a unifying thread in the garland of flowers. I never changed during three changing states of waking, dream, and deep sleep. In order to *sink* our attention to this substratum of our being, we need to falsify the three states as "not this, not this" or *Neti Neti*. It is by using the method of *Neti Neti;* the reality is arrived at by us. It is called the fourth state of *Turiya*, from the point of view of three states, but *in reality, Turiya* is not the state, but the *substrate of the three states*. Here, M.U^2. asks us to *sink* our attention to

NEGATION OF THE THREE STATES OF EXPERIE... 59

Atman, who is not *conscious of external, not conscious of internal, not massed cognitions, not grasping everything at once*, and *not inert matter*.

Atman, made up of *pure consciousness* or *Nirvishesh Chaitanya*, is the essence of knowledge and non-dual. Three states of experience are superimposed on this *Atman* of the *essence of knowledge*. It is impossible to think of *Atman*, but our thoughts are made of him. Speech cannot utter it because it is not reachable or objectified by the word. *The mind can't objectify atman.* *Atman* is ungraspable by senses. *Atman* cannot be empirically transacted because subject-object distinction does not exist in *Atman*. *Atman* has no distinctive marks. Atman cannot be seen but is the *seer*. *Atman* is eternally peaceful or can't be perturbed, happiness itself, and non-dual.

As soon as the false notions are negated about reality, the illusion created by it disappears, and the substratum is known *at once*. All changing three states are negated, and then the totally different *unchanging* and *non-dual* atman is recognized as the *substratum of all the states*. *Atman* is *Avayayam*, meaning it does not lose its nature at any time. *Atman* is a *changeless essence of the knowledge* who is *always present*, and the only *constant element in our experience*. *Atman* is the s*elf of experience*. *Atman* is *always present and knowing*, never appears or disappears.

The three states change and negate each other, hence *unreal*, while the *common substratum* continues and never changes its nature, and that forms the *reality of the three states*. First, the unreality of the three states needs to arise at the end of inquiry in favor of their being, and then three states are recognized as the sole *essence of knowledge* or *Atman*. Thus, we have now merged and resolved waking state to dream state, dream state to deep sleep state, and deep sleep state to stateless *Turiya* or *Atman*. It is like a puzzle game, where assembling the puzzle pieces one by one completes the puzzle and gives rise to a complete and meaningful figure.

M.U[3] and M.K.[4] both describe that the same all-pervading *Vibhu Atman* or *Turiya* appears in the form of three states of waking, dream, and deep sleep. This *Atman* or reality is gradually obtained by continuing inquiry and merging one quarter or *Pada* to another until the *whole undivided truth* is realized.

Turiya or *Atman* is recognized as the essence of knowledge, where no trace of ignorance of deep sleep is present. *Turiya* is a seedless *light of lights*, beyond the *reach of cause and effect*. When the *locus of the superimpositions* is known, the superimpositions of *non-self* on the *self* resolves in the knowledge of its substratum. *Turiya* or *Atman* is beyond time, space and objects, and therefore, is limitless.

---

1. 7
2. 7
3. 2
4. 1.1

14
MIND AS WITNESS

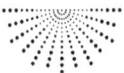

Let us come back to deep sleep. In a deep sleep, we can't find the world of objects, ego, and body. Hence, we see their non-existence or unreality. Here, the mistake that happens in interpreting our experience is that *non-existence* or nothing is the ultimate reality. Our experience consists of two essential parts, one is the knower, and the other is the known. Here, when we find a blank experience, it only means that the known part of the experience is absent, but the knower is still there, illumining the *absence of the known*. Pure *knowing capacity,* or *seer,* or *Drik* knows the *absence* and *presence* of all that was once known and now is known to be absent. M.K.[1] declares the *Drik* is pure objectless awareness to whom everything becomes the *object of knowledge,* including ego, body, objects, and blank or no objects. In the empty experience of deep sleep, resides the pure knower or seer or *Pramata*. The whole creation is negated, and only the witness as the sole reality of experience remains. Negating every concept, we come to a blank experience, as no objects. Then, negating that too, what is left is our pure *knowing-being* as the negator. Our *knowing-being* is the pure capacity of knowing or *illumining the experience,* independent of known creation. This capacity of seeing whatever is seen is called the *witness* or *Drik*. The *Drik* is *pure consciousness* only. Understand that the negator *cannot be negated. The knower can never be known.* The Brihadaranyaka Upanishad[2] asks who will know the knower? How can the knower be known?

The witness is only real because he notices the comings and goings of the three states of waking, dream, and deep sleep, but he does not come and does not go. Only the changeless one in our experience is real. Due to *remaining changeless among changing three states of experience*, the witness is called unchanging immediate knowledge, immutable mind, or *Kuthastha Aproksh Gyan*. Hence, the relational experience is nothing but the unchanging mind - the pure attributeless consciousness. Now, we have resolved the changing mind that is experienced in two extremes of active and inactive states, to the *unchanging witness*.

The pure subject that exists in a deep sleep never becomes an object of knowledge. The *Drik* or witness exists *with or without objects*. The witness is *non-relational*. In other words, when we see pure consciousness in relation to the object, then consciousness becomes the subject, and everything else or creation becomes the object. But in truth, there is no relationship between real and unreal, between truth and untruth. The establishment of this relation is ignorance of our mind about the ultimate reality, which is free from relativity, and hence absolute. Hence, pure *absolute non-dual consciousness* is called witness only *with reference to* three states which are *witnessed*.

The subject is opposed to the object is an erroneous perspective of our mind that is falsified using self-knowledge or *Atma-*

Gyan. Consequently, the subjective consciousness or *Pramata* liberates and dissolves into attributeless and subject-object duality-free pure consciousness. Known is the knower. Known's being is resolved in the *knower's being*. The *Self-evident* self is the *self-existence*: the seer and the seen merge into one non-dual awareness of the self. The subject-object duality disappears in the knowledge of non-dual consciousness or *Chaintainya Atman*.

The witness or unchanging mind gives the cognitive ability to the mind, the mind gives it to the senses, and the senses give it to the body. The capacity of knowing is witness or consciousness, which never becomes an object. By contrast, for consciousness, everything else or *Idam* becomes an object, including changing the function of mind, senses, and sensory objects. Thus, the witness is a resting and emergence place for the mind. Witness is an *unassociated self*.

We separated the *Drik* or witness in our experience from what is being witnessed or *Drsya*. Then, we found that witnessed or *Drsya* is not independent of *Drik*. Hence, we resolve *Drsya* into *Drik*. All states of experience are nothing but the *non-relational Drik*. The witness is the name of our non-dual self with respect to coming and going of different experiences, which are unreal and depend on our self for their reality. Hence, witnessed is not separate from the witness, and is the witness only.

The essence of mind is the witness only. The mind's identity is the *Advaya Atman* or non-dual self. Just as a snake appears as a string, but its actual identity is the string, the identity of the mind is the *Atman* or non-dual self. We call to mind as the mind when the non-dual self or *Atman* appears in the form of the duality of subject and object. When the dual mind rests by the *knowledge of its real nature* or identity, it becomes the *non-dual self*. We can call the self as the *non-dual unchanging original mind*. In other words, subject-object duality does not form the essential nature of our self. Our self appears in the double form of subject-object, ego, and non-ego. Then, the relational experience is born.

M.K.[3] declares that the non-dual mind *vibrates* or appears in the form of the duality of subject and object. The subject-object duality or *Grahya-Grahak Bhav* is the very *first appearance* that the witness self assumes, and then this dual mind's activities appear as *internal and external objects*. M.K[4] says the consciousness, though *motionless* because of *Avidya* when set in motion, appears as the double perceiver-perceived pair. M.K. continues and says that the real nature of the mind is *unassociated* and *objectless*. Now, we know ourselves as the unchanging knowledge that is free from any contact, and we also know that the objects do not exist.

Shiva or our self is in the form of pure consciousness. When Shiva closes his eye of pure knowledge or hides himself with his own *Maya*, creation appears, and when he opens the eye of knowledge, creation disappears.

---

1. 1.12
2. 2.4.14
3. 4.72
4. 3.29

15
WHERE THE MIND BECOMES NO-MIND

Waking, dream, and deep sleep conditions are negatable. It is the witness consciousness or *Saskhi Chaitanya* that is in the form of intellect or *Buddhi*.

We take the knower of the field (subject), as opposed to the field of awareness (object). When we refute the knower and the field of awareness, which are mistaken as *two separate parallel realities*, then we realize that the *field of awareness* is nothing but the *knower of the field*. Here, *Buddhi* or one's reasoning capacity and differentiating power ends and can't work anymore. The mind becomes no-mind. *Katha Upanishad*[1] declares that mind and senses are created or *imagined as outward going in nature* as if something *external to consciousness exists*; hence, we miss the fact of the witness lying in the form of mind and senses. *Drik* looks out as if something outside of himself and appears as waking, dreaming, and deep sleep. When *Kshetra* or field of awareness is realized as non-different from the knower of the field or *Kshetrajna*, then *consciousness recognizes itself*. I am the whole waking, dream, and deep sleep conditions. Who realizes that?

The self as pure *witness* realizes itself as attributeless, non-relative, or absolute, and the *original essence of mind*. The first step is that the mind or *Chit* appears as the *knower* of the object of knowledge *(Chit Drishyam)*. In the second step, the mind or *Chit* itself becomes an object of knowledge to the witness or *Sakshi*. *Atman* is called *Sakshi* with reference to the mind of the waking and dream state, which divides itself in *ego and objects*. Same *Sakshi* is also the witness of deep sleep. Here, the distinction between the *knower*, the *instrument of knowledge*, and the *known* disappears. We realize that it is the self that appears as them. I am *Pramata, Prameya, and Pramana*. This self is not negatable as compared to the three states. The objects are reduced to the mind, and the mind is reduced to *pure awareness* or the self. The self is *non-refutable, never changing,* and *imperishable steady knowledge*.

M.K.[2] declares that self is a pure sky of knowledge, unattached to objects and unborn or *Ajam*. It is just like the heat and light are non-separate from the sun; in the same way, the knowledge is non-separate from the self. Pure knowledge that is without the distinction of the knower, instrument of knowledge and known is not the attribute of the self but its nature.

---

1. 2.1.1
2. 4.96

16
WITNESS IS THE SELF - OUR TRUE IDENTITY

Consciousness is *Chit svarupa*, which means it knows itself. The only way to know consciousness is by being it. Rather than casting his ray of knowledge on any object, he stays as himself as *SatChitAnanda*. In the case of the self, "I am" is the subject or knower, and "I am" is the object known. Hence, both are the same person. Thus, consciousness is the non-dual knowledge and experience, where subject-object merges into one another. The realized ones express it as "I am that I am." The self is the *light of lights* by which itself and the whole of experience is illumined.

In a drama, a person became the director. Then he also played various roles in the plays and became the actor. The director, actor, and roles form the various limited adjuncts or *Upadhi* of the original person. If a person is engrossed in activities as director, actor, and roles, he suffers various limitations imposed by adjuncts. How does he realize himself? He should ask himself what was I am before identifying with any of the adjuncts. Then, he goes back from the roles to the actor, then to the director, and finally to the original and true identity of himself. Similarly, in the waking state, we need to ask ourselves what I was before identifying myself as the mind, body, and the world. What was I before being doer and enjoyer?

If we detach ourselves from the personal self and the body, what remains is the *impersonal witness self*. The impersonal witness is sheer consciousness or *Chit svarupa*. If we de-identify as the waker, dreamer, and deep sleeper, then our true self shines as *superpersonal* made up of pure knowledge. We superimposed the waker, dreamer, and deep sleeper on the true identity of ourselves as the witness self. Just like, that person has superimposed the director, actor, and roles on his true identity, and mistakes one of them as his true self. We *mistake the waker as our true self*. Our real identity is non-dual and pure qualityless consciousness or *Nirvishesh Chaitanya*. When we do not inquire into our true identity, witness becomes the *substratum of superimpositions*. Our true self is the *non-relational immediate awareness of I*. In contrast, the waker, dreamer, and deep sleeper are *relational I*. When the subject-object duality becomes true to us, our true identity as witness self is *covered* with a newborn relational identity. This relational identity changes from the waker to the dreamer to the deep sleeper. It does not stop here, but the mind divides itself further into mind and objects or *Vishay and Vishayi*. Hence, the trinity of the knower, instrument of knowing, and known *appears as real*. *Non-causality* is to see *non-separateness* of objects, the mind, and the self. No second thing exists as our true self that is *non-dual*. When we recognize the second real entity, then our self is covered by the experience, and as a result of forgetting our true self, we suffer.

The reason why suffering goes away as soon as we realize the *witness nature of the self* is that the suffering belongs to and confined to the limiting adjuncts of ego, intellect, feeling mind, senses, and the body. We de-identified ourselves with those adjuncts. We know that we are not those adjuncts, but we are non-dual, non-relational, the innermost self of all *Jivas*. Like water realizing himself as bubbles, tides, foams, etc. does not get tainted by his own modifications. The *Bhagavad Gita*[1] says that an awakened person or *Sthita prajna*, who has realized his true self stays steady, unattached, and calm amid good and bad experiences. He neither rejoices nor hates when meeting with pleasant and unpleasant experiences. The awakened one does not become afflicted by the experiences of three states. Nothing else is needed except realizing one's true *self-effulgent* self. M.K[2] declares that this is the method to cross the *Samsara* or ocean of suffering; *nothing else is needed.*

---

1. 2.56,57
2. 3.36

PART V
SELF AS WORLD

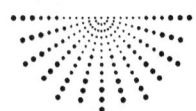

17
SUFFERING OF JIVA

As a human being, we are an embodied person with the mind and body. Our identity is solely based on the mind-body complex. This is how we know ourselves. Let us call ourselves – this conscious person whose identity is based on a mind-body complex - as *Jiva*.

M.K[1] says the peaceful and non-dual consciousness thinks himself as Jiva. Jiva imagines and feels that I am born, I am going through these experiences of life, and will eventually die. Jiva knows that I am *here*, and the world is *there*. One enormous capacity the human life has is the capacity of *doing* and *knowing*. This capacity of knowledge and work makes us proud and allows us to live a pleasant life. We can do things and enjoy things. We perform actions and reap the fruits of our efforts in terms of various pleasures. We are an enjoyer of various enjoyments that life can provide, and a proud doer of good and bad deeds. This mind-body complex based identity or Jiva is born someday and will die eventually. In between, this person goes through the best and the worst experiences of life. The Jiva has *an inner life* of which he is conscious.

The repeating pairs of opposite experiences make up the *inner life* of a Jiva. We are happy sometimes, and We are sad at other times. We are sometimes lonely and overwhelmed by the world at different times. We sometimes suffer and are peaceful at other times. We are angry sometimes and cheerful at other times. We sometimes enjoy and distaste at other times. The world is good for us sometimes, and bad at other times. Jiva tries to weed out unhappiness from his experiences and wants to keep only happiness. Jiva tries to avoid pain and suffering from his experiences, but he cannot do that. As a result, Jiva feels helpless, and his unconscious registers helplessness.

Jiva's life is a constant search for happiness and immortality. Jiva's experiences are full of uncertainty, insecurity, and fear. Jiva needs to constantly and repetitively amend the situations, relationships, and objects around him to make them conducive to happiness and security. Jiva is always tossed between pain and pleasure. Jiva regularly suffers attachment and aversion. He likes something, and he dislikes something. Jiva's object of like or dislike may be a person, situation, or even a color.

Above we depicted a picture of a relatively happy life of Jiva. Relative happiness and survival of a Jiva is subject to conditions around him and in himself. As human beings, we are limited by bodily limitations like aging, decaying, and dying. We are limited by mental deformations like attachment, aversion, envy, loneliness, depression, anxiety, anger, despair, and desire. Jiva's life is a life of continuous becoming. To become something new is a constant urge that drives the life of Jiva.

Jiva has countless desires. He continually tries to fulfill desires by performing actions to become complete. Human life is engendered by the continuous urge to act based on one's desires, which are, in turn, various attachment and aversion impressions in his unconscious mind called *vasnas*. This force of compulsion of karma is inevitable in human life. "*Karmanubandhini manushya-loke,*" says the *Bhagavad Gita*[2]. Thus, Jiva lives a life of *continuous becoming* by performing various actions to enjoy, fulfill, and protect oneself. He enjoys good and bad situations based on the result of his own actions. Thus, unconscious mind-based *vasnas* impelled desire, karma, and the results of karma forms a cycle of *sukha* and *dukha* for the Jiva. We call this bondage of cycle – *Samsara*.

Jiva needs to continually chase and acquire objects of his desire and preserve them to maintain his happiness. Jiva needs to continuously get rid of objects to preserve his happiness and security. Instant and immediate sense and ego gratification derived from objects of the world is the nature of Jiva. Objects of the world, like people, situations, and relations, are continuously changing and perishable. Jiva's blind run after objects of his security and happiness finally frustrates and disappoints him.

Fear of death and desire to complete himself is ingrained in Jiva. Being a *separate entity* from the world, fear of survival is always at the back of Jiva's head. When an unexpected situation threatens Jiva's existence, this fear of self-destruction comes out and expresses itself in Jiva's actions, thoughts, and feelings. Jiva wants more and more happiness and security. He finds happiness and security coming and going, but not staying forever. What will happen to me if I lose my job? What if I am infected by disease? Such concern for the future is always lingering in Jiva's mind.

Above is an in-depth analysis of human experience as Jiva and what we do, on what basis we do, and why we do. This is the position of ourselves as a human being bound by *Samsara*. Jiva is bound by *a cycle of birth and death*, happiness and misery, doership and enjoyership, and superiority and inferiority. Jiva helplessly suffers and is bound by the cycle of repeated actions or *karma* and enjoyments or *bhoga*. We are happy, but not enough; we are protected, but still vulnerable and can lose life anytime.

This position of ours as a human being can be compared to a sacred ficus tree, as described in the *Bhagavad Gita*[3] called *Asvattha*, with its roots upward and branches below. The tree here is a metaphor representing the ever-changing, repeating, and endless cycles of *Samsara* with a root upward and hidden.

Is there a way out of this situation as a Jiva who is a *Samsari?* Is it possible to remove sorrow and sufferings from human life? A human being who understands that his position is time-bound or continuously changing and space or body bound, understands that the world of objects or others also limits him, will try to look for the *cause* and *remedy* to the problem of *Samsara*.

---

1. 4.45
2. 15.2
3. 15.1

18
THE CAUSE AND REMEDY OF SUFFERING

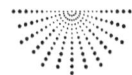

We have described the suffering of *Jiva*. When we try to find the *ultimate cause* of our suffering, we find that due to ignorance about the real nature of our self, we superimpose cause and effect on *Atman* or reality. The firm belief in *causality* arising out of *duality* is the very cause of the Jiva's suffering. How?

It is due to the attachment to the duality, Jiva becomes the agent and thinks that "I am the doer of the deeds" and "I am the enjoyer of the fruits of the actions." I should enjoy the result by performing meritorious actions and live in higher and better bodies. As soon as Jiva becomes an agent, he is *bound by* actions and its consequences. As an agent, Jiva constantly performs good and bad activities impelled by the desire due to ignorance. The result of good and bad deeds accrues to Jiva in the form of pleasure or *Sukha* and pain or *Dukha*. Thus, because of *believing himself as an agent*, Jiva is *tied* to the cycle of pleasant and unpleasant situations and suffering.

After knowing the *Atman* as seer or *Drik*, the *sense of agency* that is superimposed upon Atman is negated or made unreal. We, as *Turiya* or *Drik Atman*, see that sense of agency arises and dissolves in us. Hence, we see doership and enjoyership associated with us as *unreal*. It gives us freedom from association with *Karma* and its resultant suffering. The *Bhagavad Gita*¹ says that who understands that the self is *non-doer*, and all actions are performed by mind-body or *Prakriti* that one alone sees. The suffering of Jiva now becomes *an illusion of suffering*. How can the *unreal doer* produce the *real results*? It is the *Atman* that appears as doer and enjoyer, but he never becomes that. Like a skillful actor playing various roles, *Atman* plays the role of doer and enjoyer by wearing the robe of *doership* and *enjoyership* but knows in its heart that he is neither the doer nor the enjoyer, and has nothing to do with the *Karma* or actions and its *Phala* or fruits.

The cause of the vicious cycle of birth and death of Jiva is due to the strong identification with the *belief in the cause and effect principle*, which is solely based on ignorance *in the form of duality* about the causeless, non-dual, and unoriginated reality of *Atman* or *Brahman*. M.K.² declares that the chain *of birth and death* or *Samsara* of Jiva can't be broken until this false belief in causal law is refuted by seeing the truth of non-dual *Atman*. As long as we believe in duality, it *becomes true*, and cause and effect will continue working.

We continuously desire various objects and run after them to achieve, maintain, and want to get rid of some objects. Why? It is due to the persistent belief of two parallel realities of *mind and its objects*. M.K.³ declares that it is because of *attachment to the unreal* that our mind rushes after objects. The disastrous result of this blind run of ourselves to the objects of desire is that it hides the innate and natural happiness of *Atman*. M.K⁴ declares that *Atman* is *covered* due to its grasping of the object,

THE CAUSE AND REMEDY OF SUFFERING

and sorrow is projected. A *sense of lack or want* is ingrained into the nature of Jiva because of the *adherence to the belief in the duality* of *mind and its objects*. Because of ignorance or *Avidya*, we *locate happiness outside of ourselves* and look for objects and people who can complete us in terms of happiness and love. We project our demand for happiness upon the objects, people, and relationships around us to make us pleased. We endlessly try to complete ourselves by fulfilling various desires, but perfection always eludes us.

Seeing ourselves as an individual based on the mind-body complex is the *gross error* resulting from the root ignorance or belief in duality. *Atman*, which is *Drik* or witness in nature, is wrongly believed to be owning the mind-body or equal as mind-body. Hence, we become an embodied individual or Jiva with personality. M.K[5] declares that *Sanghatas* or aggregates like body, *prana*, or breath, etc., are unreal and depend upon Atman for their existence. Because of our association, identification, and attachment with unreal aggregates of the mind-body, we think, feel, and act as an embodied being or individual.

M.K[6] says that the limitless *Atman*, like the sky, appears in the form of embodied beings, like a space enclosed in the pot. After the destruction of the pot, the pot space appears to merge in the total space. Similarly, after the destruction of ignorance about the aggregates of body-mind, in other words, knowing their unreality, Jivahood appears to merge as the non-dual universal *Atman*. It is the attachment to the unreal that keeps Jiva bound to *Samsara*.

After knowing the bondage of Jiva, the remedy is already known. The remedy is to see the truth about *Atman* because the *cause is in the form of ignorance* about *Atman*. It is by knowing the real nature of *Atman* that appears in the form of three states of experience that relieve us from the suffering. M.K[7] declares that all suffering ends in non-dual *Atman*, who is the Lord, all-pervading among all entities, and whose nature never changes or *Avyayam*.

Jiva was under the longtime spell of twofold *Avidya:* not understanding the real identity of himself and understanding himself as something other than what he is. M.K.[8] declares that Jiva wakes up who slept under the spell of *Maya* without beginning and finds himself as non-dual *Atman*, not born, and without dream. Where is the *Samsara* now? Previously as well, *Samsara* was not there from the start. However, Jiva was under the spell of *ignorance and error* about the reality, suffering *Samsara*, like a bad dream. When the non-causal and non-dual self is realized, Jiva is released from the *Samsara*. Persistent belief in duality is the cause of *Samsara* for Jiva and nothing else. *Samara* is removing what is already removed, and the liberation is gaining what is already attained. In other words, awakening means that Jiva recognizes his innate and unborn freedom.

What happens to the awakened one? It is like a prisoner is not happy even if he is given food and shelter because he is bound by the prison walls and not free. Even though the jailer is moving in the same prison walls as a prisoner, he considers himself free. Similarly, Jiva remains bound as a prisoner of experience due to the ignorance of duality, feels himself as a *Samsari*, and suffers. When awakened to the truth of the non-dual and unborn self, he breaks forth the

THE CAUSE AND REMEDY OF SUFFERING

walls of suffering and feels and finds himself *free* even in the midst of the experience. The experience of three states does not bind him anymore; on the other hand, the experience becomes his manifestation or means to reveal himself. The awakened one moves freely in the experience of the three states without being affected by it. The awakened one is like a fish moving in a sea untouched by the currents of the water.

Jiva rests in decayless peace. He remains enlightened always without any trace of ignorance. He feels himself without wanting or desire, ever complete in himself or *Purna*. He becomes griefless, relaxed without worry and free from sorrow. Because of the recognition of the non-dual self, Jiva becomes free from grief, seeking, and fear. He becomes fearless in a real sense after seeing the truth of non-dual self-shining *Atman*. M.K[9] declares that realization of omniscient, unborn, and non-dual *Atman* is the *highest happiness* or *Ananda* itself, which is indescribable, liberation in itself, and not separate from the knowable unborn self. The awakened one experiences the *highest happiness* beyond the subject-object relationship, the cessation of all his miseries, and the Jivahood or his identity resolves as the *Bhraman-Atma*.

Fear of survival or loss of existence due to another is born of duality. Why would a person with non-dual knowledge fear or protect himself from others or the world? *Chandogya Upanishad*[10] declares that the knower of the non-dual self crosses sorrow. Countless external and internal events can make Jiva unhappy. One can't remove sorrow without *non-dual recognition of the self*. A highly civilized and educated person whose character is perfect cannot remove fear and sorrow because it is built within *human limitation*. Only knowledge of the non-dual, unborn, and unlimited self can remove human being's fear, sorrow, and seeker status.

M.K[11] declares that all Jivas are naturally pure, ever enlightened, free from any bondage, or ever liberated from the beginning. In other words, Jiva to *Atman* is a symbolic journey.

---

1. 5.30
2. 4.55,56
3. 4.79
4. 4.82
5. 3.10
6. 3.3
7. 1.10
8. 1.16
9. 3.47
10. 1.3.1
11. 4.98

19
NON-DUAL SELF AS THE WORLD

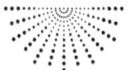

We have resolved the world made up of the multiplicity of static objects of matter into concepts. We have reduced the concepts to ever-changing modifications of thought processes or mental functions of the mind. We have then reduced the changing subject-object qualified mind to the objectless blank state of *Sunya* or emptiness. Finally, we have reduced empty blank objects or the inactive state of mind to the all-being witness made up of pure consciousness, non-dual, and unborn. We have found and recalled our original identity as "I am unborn that non-dual *Atman* of pure unqualified consciousness or *Nirvishesh Chaitanya*." Now, we traverse back and know that an inactive and active mind and its variety of objects are nothing but the non-dual *Atman* or "I am" appearing as the variety of multiplicity and diversity. We analyzed the necklace, ring, earrings, etc., and saw after analysis that they are nothing but gold only. Now, when we see a necklace, a ring, an earring, etc., we know that they are appearances of the original substance, gold only.

Only self exists and is real. No second entity is real. No second thing exists other than the non-dual self or *Advayam Atman*. When we admit the second thing as real, then the self becomes limited, and the desire, sorrow, and fear will take over us.

The *Chandogya Upanishad*[1] declares that one who does not perceive, think, hear, etc. another, is unlimited self or *Bhuma*. In contrast, the one who perceives, thinks, hears, etc. another is limited or *Alpa*. The limited one is mortal and unhappy, while the unlimited is immortal and happiness itself. We can verify that in our experience of dream and deep sleep. The whole dream universe, including movement, entities, and my dream identity, was nothing but me. M.K[2] declares that unmoving, unborn, and objectless consciousness appears as *movement*, *origination*, and *various objects*. When the universe did not exist in deep-sleep, I was still there non-dually present. In other words, the identity of the universe is the non-dual, unborn, and *essence of knowledge* self.

The Non-dual *Atman*, because of our perceiving duality, appears as the multiplicity of different Jivas - the embodied beings and the various objects of matter and mind. Because of differences in bodies, we see many beings, while in reality, they are unborn non-dual Atman. M.K[3] declares that the duality exists only empirically because it appears and behaves *as if real*. Just like because a toy elephant behaves in the way a real elephant *behaves* and *looks like* an elephant, we call it an elephant, but we know that it really did not exist in the first place.

After non-dual knowledge, our seeing or the mere appearance of phenomena does not correspond to its actual existence or *being real*. We see or *experience* the sun rising and setting every day, but *our knowledge* of this phenomenon is that the sun never rises or sets. Now, while seeing or *experiencing* duality and multiplicity, we know that it is me - the nondual *Atman* appearing as the duality and multiplicity. Although the objects and beings are different, their *essence* is the same and non-dual. We clearly know that differences are in *adjuncts* and their attributes, not in the real non-dual essence. Whether we see the multiplicity of waking and dream states or the empty state of deep sleep, we see both as one and the same reality. In the midst of the multiplicity of beings and inanimate things, we can claim that only the non-dual self - "I am" exists. The non-dual consciousness or self appears as duality and multiplicity of the world. Vedant realizes the self or *Atma* as the self of all or *Sarvatma* in its full splendor. Then, one can say that "I am" everything. I am the self of all. I am the self of the universe or *Aham Idam Sarvam*. In the presence and absence of duality, we recognize the *always present* and *ever conscious* unlimited self. The world and variety are in changing name and form only; its essence is me, always unchanging and same. This vision is the recognition of the *Atman* everywhere and all the time.

I am, being the self of everything, nothing is separate or independently exists apart from me. I am the *birthless, deathless,* and *decayless Atman,* neither subject to increase and decrease. I am the sun, moon, stars, mountains, rivers, planet, animals, human beings, insects, plants, stone, etc.: the entire creation of animate and inanimate objects. I am the waking state, the dream state, and the deep-sleep state and beyond. I am the truth or *self of experience.* I am *Brahman.* I am in the form of knowledge and ignorance. I am the cause and the effect. I am the doer, the enjoyer, hearer, perceiver, eater, feeler, thinker, and desirer. I am the subject and object. I am the ego, reason, feelings, senses, breath, and body. I am the deed, desire, emotion, food, sound, and thought. Without me, nobody can say "I am" or "I exist and know." I am the self of all or *Sarvatma*. I am the pure consciousness and the nature of the *light of knowledge* by which I know myself and the world as myself. Nothing *shines* before me and is independent of me. I shine as everything. I am the love in all relationships of every kind. I am full or *Purna*. I am the non-dual one who is in the form of multiplicity, diversity, and duality. "I am" the world.

---

1. 7.24.1
2. 4.45
3. 4.44

20
VISION OF SAMENESS

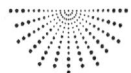

After seeing the self as the world, how does our way of living become? What is the implication or impact on our thoughts, feelings, work, and relations towards the world, after the vision of sameness or *Samatva Darshna* develops?

M.K[1] declares that the *vision of sameness* develops by recognizing that *one's self is the same self of all beings*. The most natural way of living after realizing the "self as the world" is *loving all beings* and *oneself*. Why? Because one has this profound vision of the *identity of self in all beings*. One who realized himself as all beings will naturally work for the *good of all*. Because he *sees himself in all*, he works for the *welfare of the world*. He does not work anymore for his personal self but the well-being of everybody. The *Bhagavad Gita*[2] declares that the already realized ones, and those who want to attain this vision, always works for the *welfare of all beings*. This recognition of the same self in all beings turns a human being into a saint and seer.

M.K[3] declares that the *narrow-minded* ones see the separateness of beings or Jiva, and those can never realize the natural purity of the self. The *Bhagavad Gita*[4] says that the non-dual

Self is *indivisible*, but appears as if divided among living beings. As a person with a mind, body adjuncts, one cannot be the same as others. A wooden chair and wooden table look different in name and form. If divested of name and form, the wood, or in other words, the essential self, is recognized as the same in both. Although personality differs from one being to another due to mind and body differences, their essential, innermost and bare self, which is *Atma* or self-evident *Ishvara*, is identical in all beings. I am the non-dual self before any personality adjuncts. After gaining this self-knowledge, I cannot have contempt, hate, dislike, disdain, anger, or other ill feelings, thoughts, wishes, and actions for myself or others.

Only a peaceful person can distribute peace to the environment and nobody else. Developing the vision of sameness is the most excellent service to humanity and oneself. Stabilize in the *Advait* or non-dual vision and contemplation, and then immerse in thoughts, desires, and various activities of the world. This way of thinking and living is the absolute best for all human beings because it takes one to the highest destiny reserved for human beings called liberation, joy, peace, and immortality.

A sage has always been established in the shared reality of beings. The sage knows that I am the self of everything; nothing is separate or independently exists apart from me. The sage sees the same self everywhere in everyone. Hence, the sage is internally free from complexes and intimate with every human being. He loves everybody, including animals, plants, human beings. Everybody loves him because he can resolve differences between entities and make them feel the common bond of love or *shared being* among them. A sage is universal in the clad of an individual. His thoughts, feelings, and deeds are universal and work under the vision of sameness and unity of all beings. A person with the knowledge of non-dual self or *Atman* can resolve differences of race, religion, sex, nationality, color into the unity of *Atman*. He shares happiness and miseries of others because all *Jiva* or beings are his self only. He never hurts others, and the quality of *Ahimsa* or non-injury is his nature. Compassion, selfless love, and selfless work become spontaneous in his personality without any effort to cultivate them. He responds to the world with compassion, understanding, and love. He directs others to achieve the highest goal of humanity as the realization of non-dual self.

He harmonizes and unifies the environment wherever he goes. Even the beings of violent nature become mild and loving while he is around. He is a personification of peace, love, fearlessness, and harmony resulting from non-dual self-realization. The *Bhagavad Gita*[5] says that the man of steady intellect who has realized non-dual self remains satisfied in the self, leaving all desires of the mind. The *Bhagavad Gita*[6] says that the man of steady intellect, who has realized non-dual self, wanders freely, giving up all desires for sense gratification, ego, mineness, and attains supreme peace.

A sage guide and inspire by suggesting, implementing improvements, activities, and programs leading to this vision, and establishing this vision in a human being. M.K[7] declares that let us bow down to such non-dual vision and sages who personify this unborn, all-knowledge, and multiplicity free vision of non-dual self. Let us bow down before our non-dual self, recognizing as the Ishvara, who is the *self of all*.

---

1. 4.93

2. 5.25,12.4
3. 4.94
4. 13.17
5. 2.55
6. 2.71
7. 4.100

PART VI
YOGA

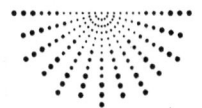

21
CONTROLLING THE MIND

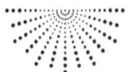

Why do we need to control the mind? What is the necessity or place of *Yoga* in our life? Why do we feel happiness and peace after controlling the mind?

It is the mind that is responsible for duality. As soon as we wake up, our mind rushes to its internal or external objects, and this goes on until we sleep. The mind's business with the objects continues even in the dream. So many times, our experience says that we could not sleep because of some strong recurring thoughts, emotions, perceptions, and memories. This world consisting of duality and multiplicity is the *expression of our mind*. By controlling the mental currents of various tendencies rushing towards its objects, we can get into a state of *mindlessness* or *Amani Bhav*.

The mind's *habit of contemplation of its objects* makes us deluded and suffering. The *Bhagavad Gita*[1] declares that the mind, when pondering on objects, becomes attached to objects, then desire for objects arises, and then from the desire, anger arises. It is the mind's *constant dwelling on objects* that results in losing our innate peace and happiness. Without our control, the mind overwhelmingly rushes towards the objects of its like that promises security and happiness. The mind retracts from objects that it does not promise happiness and security. But both attachment, aversion, and its resulting tendencies are *hiding the self* because the mind becomes outward. Hence, both attachment and aversion of objects are hiding innate peace, happiness, security, and immortality of ourselves. Whether the mind moves towards its objects of happiness or turns back from the objects of its hatred or dislike, we lose the self and experience misery at the very end of it.

It is the *dual mind* that is moving in the form of the subject-object that is responsible for the cause of suffering or *Samsara*. Hence, we need to restrain the mind from moving towards its objects by some means. This restraint of the mind is called *Yoga*. We, as human beings, are an identity based on mind and body and determinations of the mind controls us. Those who do not understand the need for controlling the mind do not really know the way to happiness and security. The mind is a bundle of desire and thoughts. We need to empty our mind from its desires, intense emotions, thoughts to find peace. We need to discipline the mind. Like when we stop fueling a raging fire, it quiets.

Through the control of the mind, our *fear and suffering* can be ended. We can get awakened and get lasting peace. The *Bhagavad Gita*[2] says that *Yoga* of controlling the mind aims to permanently cut down our association with miseries. The most important observation of our experience is that we do not experience suffering in deep sleep when the mind ceases and does not function. When the mind is present, only then duality is experienced and therefore resultant suffering.

M.K[3] declares that all mobile and immobile dual objects, including everything that is imagined and seen by the mind, are the mind alone. Why? Because the duality is never experienced when the mind's activity stops. The dualistic and pluralistic universe is the cause for our miseries, and the mind is the cause for the dualistic and pluralistic universe. Hence, control of the mind becomes a crucial and valuable effort to attain what every human being wants to achieve - peace, happiness, security, and immortality.

---

1. 2.62
2. 6.23
3. 3.31

22

RESTRAINT OF MIND USING SELF-KNOWLEDGE

*T*he restraint of mind is the most crucial goal for seekers of the ultimate reality as well as for an average person. Why? Because only control of the mind can provide us relatively stable peace, happiness, and security and paves our path towards ultimate knowledge, happiness, and immortality to fulfill our existence as human beings.

We can broadly categorize two types of methods for controlling the *disperse mind*, which is under the spell of delusion, attachment, and aversion. Our mind is overwhelmed by the world experience; it wants to find the way out. The first method of mind control is a mechanical one. This method is also important initially, but not after the mind gains relative stability and can stay on a chosen object for some time. This method is necessary to build relative strength of mind and to make the mind more concentrated. It is opposed to the mind drifting away in all directions towards different objects.

M.K[1] declares that emptying the mind using mechanical methods is like emptying the sea drop-by-drop using the blade of a grass. Even after the continuous effort of suppressing mental tides or *Vritties*, we will bounce back and forth between despair and happiness. Such is the *compulsion or habitual nature of mind*. In the Bhagavad *Gita*[2], *Arjun* declares that subduing the mind is as difficult as subduing the wind because the mind is by nature restless, powerful, and obstinate. After considerable effort, we can find that it is impossible to control the mind using mechanical methods. However, it does make a fickle mind capable of staying on a chosen object for a length of time.

The second method of controlling the mind is the winning and infallible method in which the *mind becomes no-mind or AmaniBhav*. That is the *restraint of the mind through self-knowledge*. When the mind finds out its real nature, it loses itself and becomes the non-dual self or *Atman*. M.K[3] declares that the mind stops *imagining and projecting* because of recognition of the truth of its *non-dual self*. The mind becomes free from cognizing because there are no objects to cognize like *fire without fuel*. The mind becomes *no-mind* and recognized as *pure awareness* itself when restrained through the self-knowledge. The *compulsion of the mind* goes away, and the mind is destroyed or becomes no-mind.

We can't control the mind using mechanical means because those mind practices are based on believing the *mind to be real and existent*. Only the *knowledge of reality, Self-Knowledge*, can control the mind. The mind's identity or truth is the non-dual self or *Atman*. The mind and its activities are *Atma-Brahman or Chaitanya*. The nature of the mind is the *witness self*. The *Bhagavad Gita*[4] declares that one's intellect recognizes absolute happiness as his own nature beyond perceptions of senses and mind. After the recognition, one does not move away from the truth of non-dual *Atman*.

Let us say imagine that we encounter a snake in the dark. We have two options here, either try all to save ourselves from the snake or properly look at the snake with a flashlight. If we take the first option, the snake will remain as a snake. The snake will never disappear and will remain as the cause of our constant fear and troubles. While knowing the darkness, if we adopt the other option, the snake will vanish in the rope forever on which it is projected due to *ignorance of the seer*. The mechanical method to control the mind is like resorting to the first option. While in the second option, the *mind's identity is resolved to the non-dual Atman* or *SatChitAnanda*. It is the non-dual self that appears as the dual *subject-object* or *Vishay-vishayi* mind.

---

1. 3.41
2. 6.34
3. 3.32
4. 6.21

23
MEDITATION ON ISHVARA

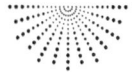

*O*ur mind continuously thinks in terms of cause and effect. Our mind can't directly and magically realize its true nature. The mind needs support or *Alamban* to reach its final goal. We need to *consciously prepare* our mind to lift ourselves to the non-dual vision of self. Our mind flow rushes in all directions to different topics and objects. First, to make the mind be able to dwell upon a single subject for some time is *a necessary step*. The meditation is withdrawing the mind from different directions, channelizing it to a chosen topic or subject, and letting it flow around the same common subject or topic for some time. The mind should not be allowed to jump all over through the diverse paths of the mind.

Because the mind wants to find out the cause of the universe that we see and experience, it is *natural to meditate* on *Ishvara - the cause of the universe*. As the mind is *receptive* in nature, it is recommended that it should be focused on *Ishvara*, a chosen deity - the *cause of the universe*. The cause of the universe means from which the universe takes birth, into which it dissolves, and by whose support it is sustained. The *Bhagavad Gita*[1] says to put one's mind in *Ishvara with qualities*, or *Sagun Brahma*. The mind sees things in terms of its qualities.

In order to make a fickle and dispersed mind gathered and stable, the chosen center of focus of the mind must have the best qualities, which is ultimately God, a deity, *Ishta* Devata, or incarnations of God such as Krishna, Rama, Jesus, or Buddha. Because the mind is receptive, its thoughts, sensations, emotions, and perceptions start flowing around *Ishvara* with qualities that the mind can think, feel, and perceive. If *Ishvara with human form* is chosen as the mind's focal point, then the mind will be able to think, feel, perceive, and sense the glory and attributes of Ishvara. Ishvara is described as the treasure of the best qualities. The mind is capable of not only meditation, but also of absorbing Godly qualities like compassion, love, truth, non-violence, service, and dispassion. Meditation is called here as a mental worship to Ishvara or *Upasana*. If one regularly performs the prescribed meditation, one's concentration not only becomes stronger, but the mind becomes purified of ill-feelings like anger, hate, jealousy, envy, attachment, and aversion.

Purification of the unconscious and *maturity of emotions* is the most significant outcome of *Bhakti* of *Ishvara with attributes*. Only *Bhakti* or meditation of mind on Ishvara can *affect and purify the unconscious mind*. The meditation on Ishvara affects and shapes a person's conscious behavior. Our mind is subjected to depression, anxiety, loneliness, and anger on trivial matters. Drugs and pills can help, but cannot remove the underlying cause in the unconscious. Only *Bhakti* or meditation on Ishvara can remove the cause because *Bhakti* connects a human being to the indwelling cause of the universe. The person doing regular meditation on Ishvara with attributes develops as a devotee or *Bhakta*.

A person with troubled feelings and thoughts needs first to make its mind stable and relatively calm using meditation. Such a person's ego gets diluted because *Ishvara* is his father and mother. Such a person is cooperative, understanding, accommodative, and can easily mix with others, and lives a life of bringing belongingness, warmth, intimacy, and love to the world. *Bhagavad Gita*[2] declares that such a Bhakta has no hatred for all beings, friendly, compassionate, without possessiveness, without doership, forgiving, and composed mind in pain and pleasure.

One cannot become happy by the possession of wealth, health, family, fame, and power, but by an *emotionally* and *intellectually matured mind* purified by meditation. A human being experiences through the mind because the mind is acting as an instrument of experience. If the instrument of experience is agitated, or full of conflict and turmoil, whatever one experiences will be an unhappy experience. If a person is endowed with an *unhappy mind*, nothing matters. The best situations in the world or even heaven will trouble the person. The meditation of the mind means creating a relatively happy, free, and secure mind. The meditation done on *Ishvara* will develop a *sensitive* and *strong* mind. The *Bhagavad Gita*[3] gives the example of a person with a steady mind, whose mind is under his control, which is called *Atmavan*. Like a tortoise who can willingly withdraw its limbs when it wishes to; similarly, a person with a concentrated mind can withdraw his mind and senses from its respective objects at will. Not only can he withdraw, but he can also put the mind and senses to a chosen object and can focus the mind on staying on the object for a more extended period.

The *Bhagavad Gita*[4] describes the attitude of a devotee of Ishvara or *Bhakta* about the *Karma* or action. *Bhakta* does *his duties* as an *offering* or *acts of worship to Ishvara*. Performing duties of daily life becomes a *means of worship to Ishvara* for a *Bhakta*. He carries out his duties with the understanding that he meets the universal needs by doing his duties regarding the family, society, country, and the world. Bhakta's performance of actions or *Karma* based on devotion to Ishvara becomes his means of recognizing Ishvara or *Karma Yoga*. *Bhakta* surrenders his will to the total will. *Bhakta's* mind-body become entirely in tune with the total will and hence becomes the perfect instrument for the manifestation of the total will of Ishvara. *Karma Yoga* helps us develop devotion to Ishvara or *Bhakti* and reduce our mind's *attachment* and *aversion*.

M.K[5] recognizes that our minds are of varying grades of the lower, middle, or the high categories of purity and capacity to grasp the truth. The scriptures teach the meditation on Ishvara out of compassion, to help gain the required preparedness of the mind which can perform discrimination and inquiry. The most important advantage of meditation on Ishvara results in gaining *Bhakti* or devotion, where our ego softens, knelt down, and melts down, acknowledging the higher pervading presence of Ishvara in us, which is the cause of our personality and the world. We know that the Ishvara, creator of the world, indwells us, very closely related to us, and always with us. Thereby indwelling presence of Ishvara in us gives us a life of belonging, intimacy, love, peace, security, trust, free from worries, and fearlessness. The meditation on

MEDITATION ON ISHVARA

Ishvara gives us the required preparedness of the mind in gaining the knowledge of non-dual self.

---

1. 12.8
2. 12.13
3. 2.58
4. 18.46
5. 3.16

24
READINESS OF THE MIND

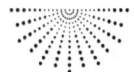

*L*et us understand the method of controlling the mind using *self-knowledge* in detail. First, let us get some prerequisites for the mind to get ready for this *yoga*.

We need to get ourselves prepared for the goal of the non-dual self. We need to relatively free us from the most disturbing passions, mainly anger, strong desire or attachment, and fear. The *Bhagavad Gita*[1] declares these passions to be the doorway to the hell and destruction of ourselves. It says further that whomever has made himself free from attachment, fear, and anger is a sage. We do not want to behave badly or improperly, but sometimes, we are being pushed by *some unknown force* against our will to act improperly. The *Bhagavad Gita*[2] declares that it is the *passion* that generates desire, which impels us against our will for improper conduct. Anger is just another form of desire. If desire is met with resistance, anger is born. Hence, we become slaves of attachment (intense desire), fear, and anger. These are our *real enemies* in the battlefield of life. Therefore, they need to be defeated, resorting to methods to discipline and turn them. We behave as a sinner or a saint based on how much we are in control of *passion born desire, anger, and fear.*

We should be *regularly studying the scriptures (Swaydhyay)* to get the sufficient knowledge to discern between real and unreal as well as to recognize which qualities are conducive to liberation and which are binding us in paving the way to freedom. For example, the *Bhagavad Gita*[3] declares few demonic qualities are false egoism, pride, attachment, anger, attachment to the bodily strength, and *ridiculing about God* or the divine in our bodies and others.

We should have the intense longing for freedom from the bondage of *Samsara* or *Mumukshatvam*. We should cultivate and adorn our character with qualities like *detachment from the objects of senses, adherence to the moral values,* or *Dharma* that makes human beings as human beings. The moral values are simplicity or straightforwardness, compassion, selfless service, leaving the fruits of our actions, non-injury, selfless love, and truthfulness.

If we have the qualities mentioned above, then it makes us an aspirant or a seeker and allows our mind to fix quickly on the goal of non-dual *Atman*. M.K[4] declares the method of contactless or *Asparsa Yoga*, which is hard to attain by the aspirants who are devoid of discriminative knowledge born of the three states. This method transcends *touch or relation* with any object. It is a pure path of non-relational knowledge beyond sensual touch culminating in the non-dual self of experience. The *Asparsa Yoga* directs Jiva or individual self to find its identity - *Shiva*, the self of all.

Initially, a person may fear to look into it because we fear losing our individual self, who is a doer and enjoyer. We fear losing our achievements, enjoyments and fear the destruction of ourselves. We never want to question our individuality due to fear of loss of ourselves and the pain associated with it. We retract back from the very place of fearlessness because of not understanding the non-dual self. Like a person keeps walking on the ground without realizing that treasure is hidden right beneath the land on which he is currently walking. We refuse to analyze our experiences with the proper scrutiny of Vedantic reason, and wrongly think that it will result in the loss of our achievements and enjoyments because of our identity as a doer and enjoyer.

---

1. 16.21,2.56
2. 3.36,37
3. 16.18
4. 3.39

25

DISCRIMINATION AND DETACHMENT

Why does the mind rush towards its objects? The uncontrollably running away of the mind's flow towards its objects forms the *distraction* or *Vikshepa* of the mind. Why? Because it does not allow ourselves to draw the mind's attention back to the ultimate reality. The task of drawing the mind's attention to the reality of *non-dual Atman* becomes as difficult as drawing the attention of a little child to some chosen object.

It is the desire or *Kama* and enjoyment or *Bhoga* that forcefully drives the mind towards its objects. Under the spell of desire and enjoyment, our mind locates happiness in the objects. We think our satisfaction and pleasure lies in the objects. Our mind thinks, if we want happiness, we must derive it from the objects, including persons that contain happiness and pleasure-giving ability. When this tendency of mind grows, it creates obsession for the objects. It makes us slaves to objects of happiness and creates mental distortions. Our mind fancies pleasure in its objects of senses and dissipates its energy.

Clearly, our mind needs to turn away from the objects and ultimately should not rise towards objects of its happiness, seeking happiness through objects, including persons.

M.K[1] declares that the mind should be turned back from the pursuit of *desire* and *enjoyment* by *non-attachment towards the sense objects,* called *Vairagya,* and by knowing that pursuing sense objects is afflicted with misery. The mind should be given reason that the objects of senses are fleeting, perishable, changing often, giving only temporary bites of pleasure, and leaving us permanently in the miserable *seeker status*. The mind should be taught that only the unborn, non-dual self *exists* and *nothing else*. *Vairagya* is the first step to thwart the mind's movement towards desiring and enjoying pleasurable objects.

The second step in reverting the mind back to reality from its dwelling to unreal objects is practicing constant discrimination between real and unreal or *Abhyasa*. The practice of repeated pondering of mind over the truth of *non-dual Atman* is what differentiates the Vedantic method of Yoga from the mechanical methods of Yoga. The mind's *process of inquiry* should be continued until it realizes its identity with *Atman- Brahman*. If our mind rises towards external objects again, we should bring it back to *contemplation* of the *real versus the unreal* by using the learning of three states experiences as the datum.

This exercise of *repeated detachment* and *discrimination* needs to be continued until we reach the goal of *non-dual Atman* through the unification of learning derived from three states of experiences.

The *Bhagavad Gita*[2] declares that our mind can be controlled using detachment and repeated contemplation on reality, which is otherwise hard to control.

1. 3.43,44
2. 6.35

26

OBSTACLES OF THE MIND

When practicing yoga, if the mind's main obstacles are identified and removed, then our practice of yoga can achieve the goal of realizing the mind's identity with non-dual unborn *Atman*. Which are the main obstacles in the way of a seeker of the ultimate reality?

The first obstacle is when in an active state of waking and dream, the mind rises to its external and internal objects. This obstacle is called distraction or *Vikshepa*, which we have already discussed. As a result of *understanding the truth*, the mind becomes quiet. The quiet mind does not rise towards the objects of its pleasure and desist from objects of its distaste. From the discrimination of the three states of experiences, we have *negated the reality of external and internal objects*. We have concluded that these objects are being perceived by the perceiving mind, and hence not independent of mind. The mind is inseparable from the objects. There are no two independent realities called the mind and the objects. The objects are concepts of the mind and *are the mind*. It is the persistent and strong belief in the duality of the *separate subject and object* that keeps the mind to continue to believe in the *reality of objects*. Once, through knowledge of reality, we know that objects are appearances and non-separate from the mind, then how can the mind rise towards its objects after its *cause of rising* is removed?

The Second obstacle is when the mind resorts to *Samadhi* or total passivity, and the mind becomes torpid. It is a temporal dissolution of mind or *Laya* into its seed state of ignorance. The mind wears out due to the effort and wants to lose itself in the effortless, no discrimination state. The mind relishes the bliss arising from the no exertion, worry free, and painless state like in a deep sleep. The mind wants to forget itself into the *temporary seed state*, which still contains the desire and enjoyment in an *unmanifest condition*. The mind is tired and resolves itself in pure ignorance and inertia. The mind should be aroused back from resting into this sleep by practicing *detachment* and *discrimination*. The effort here is to know the real nature of our experience, or the self, and not dwell in slumber, relishing in doing nothing. We need to resolve our mind into the *non-dual self* or *Brahman* that is the reality of the universe. In the seed state of ignorance, still, the *separate self* is latent and will manifest again. Our inquiry for the identity of our mind should continue by rousing the mind back from the state of total forgetfulness.

The active mind does not rush to its objects and also does not rest in a trance-like state of no effort, but may stay in the intermediary state of impressions left from passions like attachment, aversion, anger, etc. The human mind stores the impression of the previously enjoyed pleasures and replays it when the proper circumstances arise. This type of conditioning of the mind based on residual impressions of passion forms the third obstacle in the way of an aspirant of the contactless reality of *non-dual Atman*. This type of *conditioning, based on the stored impressions* of uncomfortable feelings and pleasure-giving memories, is what we call the *unconscious* portion of a human being. This unconscious controls the human being's conscious behaviors. If the unconscious is heavily loaded with lots of impressions of negative memories, a person feels more uncomfortable and suffering in himself. The person feels lots of pressure and tension coming from the unknown layer of his being. A person with a heavy unconscious is like a garbage bag filled up with trash and no dumpster to empty it. A light and humorous interaction with such a person often invokes a heavy and tense response. Pleasant and painful experiences left impressions on the human mind and kept getting stored in the unconscious until they get resolved. A person's behavior who has a heavy unconscious is erratic, turbulent, and sometimes violent. Such a person's personality is too selfish, quarrelsome, full of conflicts, and filled with complaints with himself and the world. For a joyous life, a person's unconscious needs to be light and not heavily loaded with a lot of unwelcome and negative impressions. For a seeker of reality, the unconscious needs to be faced with great care and needs to be resolved.

Because of these residual impressions, the mind resists going towards or *resting in* reality. The *Bhagavad Gita*[1] declares that even though the mind does not rush to the objects of the senses, the taste for sense objects remains in the memory and obstructs the mind from resting in reality. These impressions are a very stiff *inner unmanifest wall of ego* that *does not let the mind rest in its real nature*, the *non-dual self*. It happens because of the mind's interaction with the objects for a long time in the form of enjoyer and enjoyed, and doer and deed. Hence, these impressions become deeply rooted in mind. The mind needs to overcome this significant obstacle by performing *Karma Yoga* and *Upasana* or meditation on *Ishvara with attributes (Sagun Brahman)*. We should understand the importance of meditation on *Ishvara* or *Upasana*, which serves the purpose of purifying the mind from its negative, uncomfortable memories in the unconscious and concentrating the mind. This way, we can deal with the heavy unconscious, and make it light, so that the mind is free enough and available for discrimination and inquiry related to three states of experience.

When by repeated practice of *Yoga*, obstacles of our mind are removed, then, the mind transforms itself into *non-dual awareness*. *The Bhagavad Gita*[2] declares that like a lamp kept in the windless place, the mind of a *Yogi* or an aspirant does not flicker. The practice of discrimination, inquiry, and detachment based on three states of experience leads to the *culmination of our human experience.*

---

1. 2.59
2. 6.19

27
ASPARSA YOGA

Asparsa Yoga is a *non-dual experience* where the subject and object merge into *unity of self* of *pure non-dual consciousness*.

M.K[1] declares that when the mind does not arise towards the objects for seeking happiness, neither rests in the state of oblivion nor dwells in the intermediate state of impressions of the passions, then it stays in the perfectly quiescent state based on finding or recognizing its identity with *Atman* or self. Here, the mind itself becomes or turns into *Brahman or non-dual Atman*. Here, we can realize ourselves as happiness, undecaying peace, liberation itself, unborn, and omniscient *Brahman* revealing in every experience. Here, we know the unity of the knower, the instrument of knowledge, and the known. The dual mind of the aspirant loses itself into its identity of the non-dual self or pure consciousness. The reality is the *non-dual self,* which appears as the *dual mind of subject and object*. At this stage, the mind becomes the self or *no-mind*. It is the *non-dual self that is the original mind* or truth of the mind.

The self of experience, which is the object to be known, and the mind by which it is known, both *become one and the same reality*. The consciousness, first characterized by the *subject-object*, becomes the mind, then the activities of the mind appear as the external and internal objects. The mind's or *Praman's being* is recognized as the knower's or *Pramata's* being. The self-evident self is the existence of the mind. In other words, our mind was *never separated* from the non-dual self of experience. In addition, objects were *never separated* from the mind. It was the *belief in the duality* that kept the mind going and kept the mind in the state of suffering. After the realization of self of experience, where can the suffering stay? The self of suffering was the individual self, who is bound by *ignorance and error*. After knowing the reality of the non-dual self, where does the world, individual separate self, and body go? All *remain as self. Jiva and the world*, both are the same *self* only.

Asparsa Yoga is where the mind becomes no-mind and realizes its true identity as the *contactless, relationless, and objectless non-dual self*. One can see non-dual *Brahman* everywhere the mind goes. Our self is the steady and unmoving unqualified consciousness that *appears to be moving*. Our self is the *essence of knowledge*. M.K² declares that the mind is withdrawn from the duality because it is freed up from attachment, does not move to the next object, and stays as an *immutable self - the original nature of the mind*. The self is unborn, *undifferentiated*, and non-dual. Generally, the mind keeps hopping from one modification of itself as thought to another thought, feeling, sensation, and perception. For awakened ones, the self is realized as steady and invariable among different modifications of mind like reflections appearing in the mirror. The awakened one remains unmoved in the midst of experience and is called a man of steady wisdom or *Sthit Pragna*. He sees experience come and go, but he stays as is and knows the experience.

For the awakened one, his mind is not born. Why? Because finding unreality of the subject-object duality, there is no cause left for the mind to be born. M.K³ declares that the mind that understands *non-causality* is not born, and that itself is liberation. The mind remains as *non-dual and unoriginated*. But it was the real nature of the mind even before getting non-dual understanding. Everything seen or experienced in the present, past, and future is nothing but the *appearances of the objectifying activities of the mind*. The mind is an objectifying power of consciousness non-separate from consciousness. Inner to all that can be objectified is the non-dual and unborn self or *Atman* - the truth of mind or *objectifying power*.

Liberation or *Moksha* of ourselves from birth and death, pleasure or *Sukha* and pain or *Dukha* occurs here, and not after our death. The liberation is nothing but the realization of the eternally free, unborn, pure conscious nature of the self. Liberation is to know what we are already. Nothing new is to be gained from somewhere, but *knowing the true nature of our being* is called *liberation*. The person who *knows the self becomes the self*. Liberation is *here and now* in the same life that I am living. Why? Because the self is already known but wrongly. As a result, it appears as an individual self who is bound by *Samsara*. Liberation is the true nature of the self. Once a person becomes aware of it, he is called *Jivan Mukta* or liberated in the same life. M.K⁴ declares that the *destruction of the veil of ignorance*, called liberation, is a very natural *figurative effort* for us because we are already ever illumined, absolute knowledge, eternally free, and pure by our very nature.

The self is very well ascertained since the beginning. I know that "I am" without the help of the mind. The self, being *before the mind*, can't be known through the mind like other objects. The self is *always revealed* and never needs to be revealed through knowledge. The reason is that the self is of the nature of self-revealing or *Swayam Vibhati*. Self is the absolute knowledge, and source or real nature of mind. The mind realizes that the object to be known is already non-separable from itself. The mind loses its position that the known object must be separate from itself - the subject as opposed to the object position. The mind *knowingly disappears* in its source. The *self to be known and the knowledge* are *inseparably one* and the same entity. *The self can be known only by being it.* The self is the *non-dual, non-relational, immediate knowledge,* where all differences of doer, power of doing, deed and knower, known and knowledge disappear.

The mind is resolved in the self by the practice of *Asparsa Yoga*. M.K[5] declares that there is no grasping or giving up of any objects as the self is beyond thought, and established as the self that is the pure, *changeless knowledge*. The self is where speech and mind does not function. It is beyond all expressions, without fear, peaceful, and pure consciousness by nature. When fuel is exhausted, then fire is extinguished. Similarly, with all its functions, the mind loses itself into its real nature and stays as the *original person* or self.

---

1. 3.46
2. 4.80
3. 4.77
4. 4.98
5. 3.37,38

28
THE SELF AND EMPIRICAL EXPERIENCES

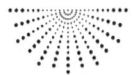

The self is non-dual consciousness, and empirical experiences are *its appearances*. We need to understand the relation between the self and the empirical experiences that we are going through every day and will continue to go through during our whole life. We need to see if any relation exists between the consciousness and its appearances. This is a key to understanding the problem of human suffering interwoven in the form of empirical experiences.

I am born, going through experiences of this life, and will die at some point in time. I am happy. I am unhappy. I am lonely. I love you. I hate you. The world is terrible. The world is good. I am angry. I am suffering. I am enjoying the world. I am jobless. I am black. I am white. I am a sinner. I am virtuous. He is mean. He is good. I feel insulted. I am depressed. I am weak. I am not good. I am the best. I am a woman. I am a man. I am old. I am fearful. I have anxiety. I am peaceful. I am a doctor. I am African. I am an American. I am an Indian.

From our few experiences above, the self seems affected by the good and bad experiences. The self appears to be born and also appears to be dying. Our life is mixed with happiness and suffering. Pleasant and unpleasant experiences of life make us delighted and depressed. The self seems to be dancing on the tune of empirical experiences and experiences pain and pleasure. That means we can say that empirical experiences are the cause of happiness or suffering of the self. We keep trying everything in our hands to see ourselves pleased and happy.

We have already established that our nature of self is non-relational, non-dual, and cause-and-effect relation free. But that is contradicted by empirical experiences that we are going through. That is because we have attachment and identification with our belief that the self is dual and is affected. Our faith in duality and causality is the cause of our suffering. Once we find out that there is no relationship between self and the empirical experiences, then we stop superimposing the cause-and-effect relationship on ourselves. The self is non-dual and without association or *relationless*. We see the contradiction because of the strong adherence and taking for granted our present experience as they are without discriminating them under the scrutiny of Vedantic reason using all three states of experience.

M.K.[1] gives an example of a firebrand. Let us take a similar example of a sparkler. When a sparkler is moved with our hand, it makes circles, lines, etc. figures. We see marvelous displays of various figures. When we stop it, all figures go away, and we simply see a still sparkler. When the sparkler was moving, we saw multiple figures. From where did these figures come? When the sparkler was still, where did these figures go? We say that really, these figures did not come out of a sparkler, and never disappeared in the sparkler because the figures were *the appearances* caused by the movement of the sparkler. The appearances are without material or *substance-less*, and hence coming to creation and going to destruction *does not apply* to it.

Similarly, when pure non-dual consciousness is moved by or superimposed with the root ignorance, then it projects subject-object difference as its first appearance. Then, the whole of the empirical experience consisting of the knower, known, and knowledge emerges. In the waking and dream state, when the mind is active in the form of subject-object duality like a sparkler moving, then the empirical experiences are formed like the figures of the sparkler. When the mind is at rest, like in a deep sleep, we do not experience anything. These empirical experiences are *reality-less* or *non-substantial* and depend on the self for its existence and sustenance. Only if empirical experiences consist of their own reality, then only they can relate to or *affect* the Self. The mind as the *subject-object duality* is the *first appearance* of the self. Pure, immutable consciousness seems to be moved or *throbbed* and giving rise to empirical experiences.

The empirical experiences are mere appearances of the non-dual consciousness, and therefore consciousness is not their cause, and they are not its effects. We cannot define the cause-and-effect relationship between two orders of reality, where one is real, and the other is an appearance of it or an illusory superimposition on its substratum. For example, a rope is hanging from a tree in the dark and mistakenly perceived to be a snake. Here, the snake is not caused by rope; it is superimposed on the rope by the ignorance of the seer. Moreover, the snake does not emerge from the rope, and neither is going to disappear in the rope. Why? Because the snake is "seen only." Similarly, empirical experiences are not coming out of the consciousness and do not sink back to consciousness. The nature of appearances is neither existence (*Sat*) nor non-existent (*Asat*). They are *unthinkable or illusory superimpositions* on the substratum.

We see that a substance can cause another substance, or an attribute can cause another attribute. Our inner self is neither a substance nor an attribute. The non-dual self is *part-less* as well as not an attribute, and hence cannot be the cause of anything. The self is pure consciousness *immutable, without a second,* and *unborn.* Our selves can't be the cause of another. We superimpose various ideas of the birth, death, movement, substance, etc., on the self. Hence, we experience that I am born, I am dying, I am moving, and I am a substance or an object. M.K[2] declares that as long as we have taken granted the firm belief and attachment in the causality belonging to ourselves, then the empirical experiences will continue affecting us. Because of this adherence, the cause and effects start working and are taken to be real.

The relation of our self with the empirical experiences must be clarified using the vision of Vedanta and directly seen by us. This vision of Vedanta is the only way to free ourselves from suffering, establish in fearlessness, feel imperishable peace, and awaken to the real nature of ourselves. M.K.[3] declares that from the relative standpoint of causality and duality, we assign birth and death to a *Jiva,* and not from the *absolute standpoint.* The kingdom of empirical experiences is illusory and impermanent because it is based on ignorance of the self. In reality, we can't apply birth and death to Jiva but only from the empirical point of view. M.K.[4] declares that it is like an *illusory sprout* coming out of the *illusory seed* in a magical show. First, we assume causality between consciousness and empirical experiences, and then we say we are born, dying, and go through various experiences of our life which are affecting us. Empirical experiences *cannot affect* our self of pure awareness. Just like the superimposed water on the sand in the desert in the midday can't drench the sand. As a result of this knowledge, we are now able to say that *I am unborn*.

---

1. 4.49-52
2. 4.55
3. 4.58
4. 4.59

PART VII
ATMAN

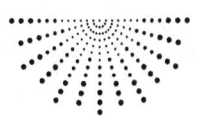

29
IDENTIFICATION WITH UNREAL AND SEEING THE NON-DUAL REALITY

*I*dentification with unreal or *Abhut Abhinivesh* creates strong attachment and insistence on the duality of subject and object. It is equivalent to losing control of the mind. The *veiling and projection* power of mind makes us suffer. It is the self-delusion or *Viparyasa* that causes bondage to an individual or *Jiva*. What is its antidote? Its antidote is seeing the non-dual reality or *Bhut Darshnat*. Seeing reality falsifies the mind and its objects. The destruction of the mind or *Amani Bhav* is realized as the non-dual self of pure consciousness. The control of the mind by understanding its real nature culminates in the limitless, indivisible, partless, modification-less, and objectless reality of the self. This self or *Ayam Atma Brahma* is the true nature of mind and world experience.

It is the *sense of reality attributed to the mind and objects* that become the cause for the suffering of *Jiva* or an individual. That is why different individual minds pursue different objects. Attributing a sense of reality creates priorities and values in the human mind. For example, for a businessman who works to accumulate profits through business, money is real, his absolute priority, the focus of all his activities, and his every breath. Once the mind sees external objects as reality, we have a strong attraction and attachment to it.

The desire for external objects binds so much that it becomes *obsession and addiction* for some objects. This strong and strange attraction towards objects not only continues throughout our life, but also it *impresses our mind* deeply. As children, we loved toys. Then we became older and social status, wealth, health, fame, power, progeny, etc. became the objects of our passion and attraction. The objects of our seeking are changed, but our mind remains in the same condition as a *seeker* and never gets satisfied. A sense of lack or want, dissatisfaction, and incompleteness continues throughout in the background of our mind. Our mind has to land on external objects, including persons, to obtain satisfaction, stay happy, and stay in a pleasant state.

When this *bound by desire* condition of ours comes to our attention, only then do we start thinking about the solution to the desire for external objects, and do we start seeking the reality which is *complete, full*, and the *whole*. We falsify through discrimination, and learning from the experience of the dream state that objects external to our mind are unreal and *depend on the perceiving mind*. Hence, they are non-separate from the mind. We learn that the mind and its objects *mutually exist* and are not independent of each other. Therefore, our mind becomes more peaceful and relatively happy in terms of *running after objects* of its desire. We stop *attributing reality to objects as external to the mind*.

Still, we're getting happy, sad, and the attraction of internal objects continues. Like in a dream, we are still feeling the same dual states of mind of being happy and miserable. Here, the objects become part of our mind, but the *subject and object division* remain reality. The mind still remains as real, and we still experience suffering like in a dream. Here, the mind creates its objects of attraction and plays around. The external objects are negated based on reality, but the internal objects including thoughts, feelings, and perceptions of smell, taste, touch, form, and sound remain real. We still feel limited by the limitation of these internal objects or activities of the mind. The mind can be in a state of despair or happiness. Our suffering continues in a subtle form as we are aware of the *reality of internal*.

When we start looking more in the *working of the mind*, we find that the mind is the always-changing and dynamic process of thinking, feeling, sensing, and perceiving in terms of five senses. The mind, in its root sense, is the *division of ego and non-ego*. This division is withdrawn every day in the deep sleep of our experience. In other words, the mind or ego and non-ego division is not a real or *permanent entity*. We find that the mind is non-separate from non-dual *Atman* or self. It was the *false existence attributed to the mind* that made us suffer and kept us mortal. The *materiality, movement, and birth* are superimposed upon the self. The subject-object duality disappears in the knowledge of the non-dual self. The self is non-dual, *made up of pure consciousness*, and is the *imperishable witness of the mind's activities*.

The witness-I know both the active state of mind and its absence. Hence, only the witness or the self is real. It is the self who projects in the form of the mind. *Not knowing the witness*, only the ever-changing *field of experience* becomes real. *Katha Upanishad*[1] declares that the outgoing nature of the mind prevents the seeing of the inner non-dual self. Hence, those desirous of immortality should discriminate, and turn the mind inward and resolve into the witness nature of non-dual self. The witness can never be known *as an object*. The self in its *witnessing function* appears as the *subject-object dual*, and the relative mind seems to be as created, but not in reality. *The unchanging witness is veiled as the continuously changing field of experience*. The seer or *Drik* name of the self also goes away once the seen or *Drishya* is realized as not independent and separate from the seer. It is with respect to the three states of our experience that the self is called the witness.

The self *pervades* every experience of the mind. The projecting power comes to an end when the self is known. *The self is known only by becoming the self*. The non-dual self needs to be recognized as the sole reality of the universe of experience. This knowledge is the true knowledge or *Tattva Gyan*, where the essence of the universe is realized as the self. Self or *Atman* is realized as *Brahman* or reality of experience. What happens when the identity of the mind is recognized as the non-dual self? The state of self-delusion comes to an end. It is the non-dual self or *Atman* that *appears* as ego, body, senses, objects, and the world.

An illusion or appearance can never affect the locus or *Adhisthana* of it. It is like a person who wakes up from the deep sleep of self-ignorance who has experienced many births, deaths, pain, and pleasures. The essence of mind is objectless or *Nirvishay*, and relationless or *Asang* means non-dual or *Advait*.

1. 2.1.1

30
NON-ORIGINATION

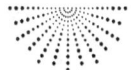

Our mind works in terms of space, cause, and time. When we look at the universe, our intellect asks what is the cause of this creation that I am seeing? Our intellect can't rest until it finds it. Even when looking at a cellphone, our intellect asks, who made it? Because I see the product or creation, there must be a maker of it. Our intellect works and is designed to see *causality*. It is useful in the practical world, where it solves our everyday issues. But, when we ask what is the cause of the entire seen creation or universe, we need not assume the practical reference of causality. We presuppose that creation is granted, and ask the question of who is the creator. In other words, we need to question causality itself. Is causality real, or a filter applied by the mind - meaning *believed only*? We need to investigate causality itself.

We are examining if there really is a causal relation between Ishvara and its creation. If *Sat* or existence is the cause, then it can't be born. Here, *Sat* or existence means always there, never to become absent, or appear and disappear. Why? Because a thing's *inherent nature* can never change. A thing cannot become other than what its nature is. Like the sun never gets deprived of heat and light. The heat and light are the sun's nature. If the pure existence is the nature of reality, then it can't slip into birth, because it already exists. If pure non-existence or *Asat* is the nature of reality, like horns of a hare, then how can it slip to birth? M.K[1] declares that then the only option left is that there is really no origination or *Ajati*. It is the non-dual unborn *Atman* that appears as the creation.

For example, if we look at the world and ask, what is the cause of the shirt? We may say fabric. Then, again we ask the same question, what is the cause of the fabric? We may say yarn. Then, again we need to ask the cause of it, and we say fiber. The finding of cause endlessly continues because there is no end to this causal chain. Take another example, what is the cause of the body? We say organs, then tissue, then its cause is cells, etc. We never arrive at the final cause, and end up in the *infinite regress* if the *cause is also born*. If we take anything in the practical world, and we see endlessness of causality. If the cause of the universe is unborn, then it can never be born, and if it is born, then we can't find its cause in turn. Hence, again we conclude the *non-origination* of the universe. M.K[2] declares that the immortal cannot become mortal, and the mortal can't become immortal as a thing can't change its nature. It is pure non-dual and unborn consciousness that appears to us as a creation.

We infer the external world as the cause of our inner experiences of pain and pleasure. We need to see and verify in our experience that the external objects are inferred by our *causal prejudice* and *given existence*. We have a sensual experience, which we see in terms of the mind's impression, and then we guess causality that *assumes* externality as real. We have already established that the outside world is mind only, and the mind is *pure awareness* or *Atman*. Realism, which takes the external world of objects as real, needs to be merged or resolved as the mind functions or idealism. Then the idealism, which takes the *mind as real*, needs to be ultimately merged or resolved in *Ajati* or non-dual witness *Atman*, who is mind and its objects. No causal relation exists between Atman, the mind, and the objects. The only identity that exists is the non-dual immutable *Atman* appearing as the dual mind of the subject-object pair, and afterward, the mind appears as objects.

M.K[3] declares that the real cause or *Sat* cannot give birth to the real effect because the cause is already there or existing. The real cause or *Sat* cannot give birth to the non-existence or *Asat* effect, because its nature as *Sat* can't change. The unreal cause or *Asat* cannot give birth to the real effect in the form of the universe that exists, because the cause is already not there or non-existing. The unreal cause or *Asat* cannot give birth to the non-existent effect. We may argue that the unchanging and immortal cause gives birth to the changing and mortal universe as its effect. It is not possible because the effect's nature can't be totally different from the cause. M.K[4] asks how the immortal *Atman* or the self can become mortal or individual Jiva? The body and ego can be mortal, but not the self. If we say mortal cause gives birth to mortal effect, then we reach the fault of *infinite regress* of the causal chain without a final cause or end, and no possibility of liberation for *Jiva*. Again, the cause cannot be immortal if the effect is mortal, denying all opportunities of liberation or *Moksha*.

We can also observe the case where cause and effect are mutually related and depend on each other. Like right meritorious

(Dharma) actions, and wrong actions (Adharma) produce birth in higher and lower species or bodies. Likewise, when Jiva is born in a body and does good and bad activities, it becomes the cause of Jiva's merit (Dharma) and demerit (Adharma). Here, the cause produces an effect, and the cause itself is born of a cause. M.K[5] says if the effect is the producer of the cause, and the cause is the producer of the effect, it is a contradiction like a father is born of a son. Also, both cause and effects are born of each other; hence, it can't be beginningless or *Anadi*. In order to establish a cause and effect relation, the cause has to be *preceded in time before the effect*. In this case, the cause and effect are either simultaneous or dependent on each other, and hence we cannot say who came first? It is like the chicken and egg situation. For establishing cause and effect relations, cause needs to precede the effect in time. Also, for events that occur *simultaneously*, we cannot establish a *causal relationship*.

From the point of view of ultimate reality, it is free from cause and effect relation. The causality is the mind functioning. Non-evolution is the truth. It is pure consciousness, non-dual self, or *Atman* who appears as the evolution. M.K.[6] declares that the four categories are being superimposed on the non-dual self, which is based on existence, non-existence, the combination of existence, non-existence, and absolute negation or non-existence. First of all, few of us see the self as the experiencer of pain and pleasure. The self is existent but different from the body as the enjoyer and the doer. Secondly, few of us see the self as impermanent, separate from the body, and equal to the intellect. The self is momentary consciousness. Third, few of us see the self exists and does not exist, different from the body, but of the same size of the body, exists in the body, and destructs when the body dies. Lastly, some of

NON-ORIGINATION

us see no self or total non-existence is the truth. All four categories are different superimpositions on the non-dual self, assuming immutability, changeability, and a combination of them.

The self of our experience is free, untouched from all the above four categories, and is *omniscient*, pure non-dual consciousness, without beginning, middle, and end, the substratum or essence on which the above four categories of different illusory views of the self is assumed. M.K[7] declares that the self or ultimate reality is free from *birth*, dream, sleep, and self-revealing. The *self knows itself* and reveals itself by itself. The self-luminosity is its very nature. The world, body, mind is revealed by the self, while the self is *self-revealing*, and in the form of pure consciousness or *Nirvishesh Chaitanya*. The self is not known by any other entity but by itself.

The self is non-dual; that means *no other entity exists* besides the self. Everything else, *other than the self* or *Idam*, is only an *appearance of the non-dual self*. The nature of self is perfect happiness and eternal peace. It is the unoriginated self that *appears* as creation. In reality, there is *no creation*; only the *self is*.

---

1. 4.4
2. 4.7,8
3. 4.40
4. 4.10
5. 4.15
6. 4.83
7. 4.81

31
FALSIFYING OWNER OF COGNITION

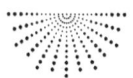

We think and feel ourselves as the owner of cognition or *Pramata*. It is the main obstacle that blocks our vision of the ultimate truth. The owner of cognition is nothing but our identification to intellect or *Buddhi*.

We can falsify the *owner of cognition* by knowing or recognizing ourselves as the *essence of cognition*. Know ourselves as "I am the essence of cognition" and not mistaking oneself as the owner of intellect or cognitive faculty.

What happens when we take ourselves as the owner of cognition? We become the *thought qualified consciousness* or *Jiva*. The pure consciousness becomes consciousness limited by the intellect or mind. The *sense of agency* arises in the pure consciousness first and divides the experience into the subject and object. It creates the *I-thought* or *Aham Pratyay*. This thought qualified consciousness is like a *reflection of consciousness* in the intellect or *Buddhi*. So first, the pure consciousness imagines *Jiva* or the individual self. The subject and object division becomes real in the individual self because of the identification of pure consciousness with the adjunct of intellect. Thus, the *I-thought* is created, and the mind becomes operative. *Jiva* made up of "I know," "I do," "I enjoy" appears.

Agency consciousness cannot be us. Why? Because it appears and disappears. The I-thought changes as a knower, doer, enjoyer, feeler, thinker, smeller, tester, etc., based on what adjunct it is associated with. We are not this momentary consciousness. We appear as temporary because of strong identification with agency-idea as the owner of cognition. When we negate the I-thought (*Aham Buddhi*) as our intrinsic nature, our *empirical experience* characterized by subject-object difference as knower, doer, enjoyer, I am happy, I am unhappy, etc., comes to an end. The Knowership belongs to I-thought and not to the self. The self is the *witness* of I-thought. When the mirror of I-thought negated by knowledge of the self, no reflections of the knower, the doer, the enjoyer, etc., comes. The self is realized as *Brahman* or the reality of the universe. The mind becomes no mind or *AmaniBhav*. The death of the experience happens upon the realization of pure consciousness or non-dual self. After that, the *subject-object difference* seems illusory even in the waking and dream state.

Going beyond agency consciousness is to know ourselves as the *essence and witness of cognition* and not its *owner*. Like one sun illuminates the whole world, the one intellect illuminates the sun, and the self illuminates all cognitions of the intellect, starting with *subject-object difference* and the *I-thought*. Know that I am that light or illumination capacity of the pure consciousness in the intellect, which forms the essence of it. The stress of intellect and emotions can't affect us after falsifying I-thought or *agency consciousness*. Know that the changing cognitions of the intellect are not my intrinsic nature, but the *chit svarupa* or "I am" made up of pure consciousness is my real nature. The self is a non-relational immediate awareness of I. The pressure in mind goes away once I-thought is negated by the knowledge of the witness self. Know that I am not the *owner of cognition*, but that I *pervade all cognition*. Without "I am" being always present and always knowing, how can cognition work? The self is unchanging, thought-free, imperishable, non-dual, and self-effulgent. When a dual mind is negated, the self-effulgent self is realized. It is like an eye is negated, where is the owner of an eye? The self is the pure *capability to know* nature or *Nitya Bodh SaktiMat Svabhav*.

We need to negate the "relational I" in the form of *I-thought*, which is the essence of a *separate person* or *Jiva*, and which is refuted in favor of *non-relational limitless I* or *Bhuma*. The self is *Brahman* or the reality of the universe. Upon refuting I-thought, the center of all complaints and dissatisfactions burns down by the fire of knowledge. Upon realizing *Brahman* or the reality of the universe, everything is realized as the *Brahman* or the self. The ego is *Brahman*, the buddhi is *Brahman*, the feeling is *Brahman*, the senses are *Brahman*, the sensations are Brahman, the body is *Brahman*, and the objects are *Brahman*. *Knowing* the *Brahman* is the *same as being* the *Brahman*. We realize that the *knowingness of the self* was never separate from the self. We understand that the object of knowledge or the self was never separate from the knowledge by which the self is known. Thus, the self is *motionless, steady knowledge* where the knower (*Pramata*), knowledge (*Pramana*), and known (*Prameya*) are one and the same reality.

The mind need not be disciplined by using mechanical practices, but to be seen as non-separate from non-dual *Atman* or self. It can be achieved by repeated contemplation, like the one we are currently doing between the real and unreal. First, the idea of agency or I-thought is denied as the true nature of the self, then the cognitive faculty or the *center of perception* is denied. As a result, the means of knowledge is realized as the being of the knower itself. Like a person standing before the mirror recognizes its reflection in the mirror.

All individual selves are one and the same self only. The individual self is none other than the mind qualified *Chaitanya* or consciousness. We avoid looking into the real nature of the self because of the fear of *self-destruction*. We fear losing our center of enjoyment and achievements and revert from the *fearless self*. We should continue our investigation into the real nature of the experience until the cognizer and cognized becomes one. The process of awakening is the process of recognizing the true self of the individual. Upon dawning of awakening to the non-dual self, *wherever the mind goes*, we realize ourselves.

32
THE EMPIRICAL AND ULTIMATE TRUTH

We need to accept mainly two categories of the truth, even though the truth is only the ultimate one. The empirical or practical truth is based on the common understanding and knowledge of the common people. The empirical truth is where we take our human experiences through mind and body for granted and conduct our everyday transactions.

The ultimate truth lies in recognizing the non-dual self as the underlying reality of our phenomenal empirical experiences and is beyond thought and speech. We realize that our empirical experiences are non-separate from the non-dual self and have no reality of their own. The empirical experiences are the projection of the universal mind, and the universal mind is a pure non-dual consciousness.

In a magic show, a magician shows a huge elephant in the cage, moving his trunk and tail like a true elephant. Then the magician makes that elephant vanish from the cage. Even though the magical elephant appears as real, the spectators know its truth but still refers to the illusory elephant as if it were a real elephant and talks about the magical feat of the magician. Here, the knowledge or the truth of an elephant differs from the elephant's empirical experience. In the same way, in our empirical experiences of the world, duality, causality, multiplicity, individuality is accepted *to conduct our daily routines*. But from the ultimate truth perspective, a man of the highest and steady wisdom knows that it is the *non-dual self that is revealing itself* in every empirical experience that we had, we can have, or we will have. Thus, there is no contradiction between practical and absolute for the realized one, but the proper tuning of practical to the ultimate truth.

Even though empirical everyday experiences appear as dual and causal, the realized one knows that the truth is non-dual and non-causal. It is like enjoying the movie or the drama without getting involved or affected by it. While living the life of a human being, the realized one is not affected by the *Samsara* or the cycle of birth, death, and suffering from pain and pleasure. Established in the non-dual ultimate truth, the realized one feels unconditional undying happiness and fearlessness.

M.K.[1] declares that having secured and realized the non-dual self, behave in the world as one of them like an unrealized one. This is because the knower of the truth knows himself as the self of all, and non-separate from the world. He does not take a superior role, but behaves, acts, feels, thinks as one of the common people, and suggests and elevates them by his speech, thought, feeling, and action towards the ultimate truth. *Bhagavad Gita*[2] declares that because the wise person is full, the desires or desirable objects entering into his mind do not disturb his peace, but instead gains the peace. It is like the rivers entering into the ocean from all sides, but the sea remains still and unchanged. One does not run after or *chase after the objects of desire* when the *Ananda* or undecaying happiness nature of the self is realized.

The realized one gains peace and moves in the dual world with *negated individuality*, without worry, and longing for the desired objects. He is free from the limited sense of 'I' and 'mine.' Although, he responds and behaves as if he is an individual in the empirical dual world. The realized one's thoughts, feelings, and actions are originating and *referencing* the non-dual self when moving in the empirical world. The realized one thoughts, feelings, and actions are revealing the non-dual self of pure consciousness in the empirical world. He has *no personality* but behaves like he does. He always works for the good of all because he sees himself as all beings and non-beings. The *Bhagavad Gita*[3] declares that a wise person is awakened to the *ultimate truth of non-duality*, while others are sleeping in the *ignorance of duality*. Because of awakening to the non-dual knowledge, the wise man *sees everything as himself alone*. The wise man is *grounded in the ultimate truth of the non-dual self*. The *Bhagavad Gita*[4] declares that the wise one sees the duality and multiplicity has its *ground* or *being* in the non-dual self, and is *projected* from the non-dual self alone.

The wise man feels harmony and sees unity in appearing diversity. He brings harmony, unity, resolution of problems, happiness, and peace to the world. While others, who are sleeping in the sleep of duality or *grounded in empirical truth*, experience conflict, fear, desire, suffering, and bring to the world division, strife, problems, suffering, and restlessness.

The *Bhagavad Gita*[5] dedicates two verses to explain the result of gaining self-knowledge which is the realization of Jiva's *innate freedom*. After gaining self-knowledge, even though Jiva is situated in the mind-body, he does not get affected by their qualities and limitations. This *path of self-knowledge* is the only means for the *Jiva* to discover himself as *Ishvar*a and, as a result, realize his *innate freedom*. This inherent freedom is what *Jiva* is always seeking for and aims for all of his various activities. By *piercing the human experience* and *establishing in the non-dual self*, the human being, while living the present life in the current mind and body, does not become tainted by the empirical experiences that he goes through. Like the all-pervading space because of its subtle nature, it is not contaminated by what appears or disappears within it.

M.K[6] declares that a human being who is firmly resolved about the self and situated in the *unoriginated sameness* is called of supreme wisdom. The man of the highest wisdom has crossed the *kingdom of duality*. The world of empirical truth is puzzled by such a person, as he leaves no track behind like the footprints of the birds in the sky.

---

1. 2.26
2. 2.70,71
3. 2.69
4. 13.30
5. 13.31,32
6. 4.95

33
ARISING OF FULLNESS

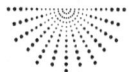

As an individual person, we are always bound by ignorance and desire. We do actions throughout our life prompted by desire. Our activities never rest except unconsciously in the night. This knot of ignorance, desire, and action veils our real nature. Our body and mind urge us to act to satisfy their unconscious urges, which can never be satisfied.

When *Jiva* gains the knowledge of the non-dual self and hence, establishes himself in that knowledge where the knower, known, and knowledge becomes the same person, his *jivahood* gets destroyed, and an *inner fullness* arises in its place. Arising of this inner fullness breaks forth the *knots of the individuality*. The fullness that arises as a result of self-realization destroys the bonds of *Karma*. After the self-realization, a wise person no longer remains under the spell of *desire and action*. He achieves the *end result of all his activities*. He finds no more reason to act on the basis of individuality, because individuality is negated by knowledge of the self, and the fullness or *Ananda* dwells in its place. All his activities express this fullness. He acts for the good of all and not for the few that he knows and feels good for. He does not rest effortlessly like in a deep sleep but realizes the true end of all activities because the ultimate result of all actions is attained. All desires of the *Jiva* are satisfied *all at once*. For such a person, no individual agenda is left to achieve. For such a person, all deeds that are to be done are already done in the knowledge of the non-dual self of fullness.

The *Bhagavad Gita*[1] declares that by knowing the secret of the non-dual self, the wise ones accomplish everything. His feeling, thinking, and actions now emanate from this ocean of fullness. After the realization of the non-dual self, one always remains complete, so never being incomplete again. His activities are not arising to complete himself, but becomes the play of fullness. Such a person's actions, thoughts, and desires are fullness playing with fullness.

Breaking forth the dense fortress of self-ignorance, desire, and action is the final goal of human life. For such a person, the *piercing of the human experience* is complete and total. As a result of this real freedom, he is called the *liberated while living* or *Jivan Mukta*. The human experience does not veil the non-dual aware self of *Jivan Mukta*, but in reverse, every experience becomes the revelation and *recognition of the self*.

M.K[2] declares that we bow down and salute to the highest destiny of all beings, which is all-knowing, free from duality and multiplicity, unborn sameness, difficult to see, and very profound.

---

1. 15.20
2. 4.100

ABOUT THE AUTHOR

Tushar Choksi is a sincere seeker of the reality of human experience since his childhood days. Due to the undercurrent force of spirituality and the desire to be a good human, he practiced meditation and studied the Vedantic scriptures for more than twenty-five years. During his life, he studied in-depth and participated in various activities based on the Vedantic tradition. One major activity he has been part of for most of his life is the activity of *Swadhyay* inspired by *Pujya Padurang Shastri Athavale*. He was also engrossed in the teachings of *Shri Ramkrishna and Vivekananda,* and the tradition of *Arsha Vidya of Swami Dayananda Saraswati*. Currently, Tushar conducts classes on Vedant and continues his study of Vedant.

tusharchoksi.com

www.ingramcontent.com/pod-product-compliance
Lightning Source LLC
Chambersburg PA
CBHW051400290426
44108CB00015B/2097